IT Doesn't Matter
—Business Processes Do

By the authors of the landmark book

BUSINESS PROCESS MANAGEMENT: THE THIRD WAVE

Featured book recommendation:
Harvard Business School's *Working Knowledge*

"Don't Bridge the Business-IT Divide, Obliterate it!"

www.bpm3.com

Why this book?

A torrent of debate ensued in the weeks following *Harvard Business Review's* May 2003 publication of Nicholas Carr's article, "IT Doesn't Matter." Numerous responses and rebuttals began pouring in from around the world, including those from the likes of Bill Gates, Michael Dell, and just about every business and technology publication on the planet, even daily newspapers.

Carr makes several accurate observations that touched a nerve in the IT industry, eliciting some sharp responses that prompted *eWEEK's* John Taschek to write, "Industry partisans who have read it but can't accept much of it as true are either awash in denial or so obsessed with self-preservation that they are blinded by the facts."[1]

By writing the article, Carr has rendered a great service to the IT industry—a wake-up call. We thank him for that, and we thank the many who have stepped up and entered the debate (see Appendix). Their insights and his have helped us to connect the dots in order to provide a more complete picture of the role of information technology in business. For although Nicholas Carr certainly created a stir, his analysis leaps from assertions about the *IT industry* to drawing conclusions about the *business use of IT* as an enabler of competitive advantage. In consequence, he is led to prescriptions that focus on the past—the *first* fifty years of the business and IT relationship—and he has missed the breakthrough that sets the stage for the *next* fifty years.

So, in the spirit of HBR Editor Thomas A. Stewart when he wrote, "Our ideal reader wants give-and-take, argument and counter-argument, the better to understand the issues,"[2] this book's critical analysis of Carr's thesis sets the record straight. It explains the breakthrough of business process management, which is the epicenter of IT going forward, and provides a message that is both urgent and critical for business leaders caught up in the great IT backlash from the Wall Street-driven overspend of the go-go 1990s.

Howard Smith
Peter Fingar
June 2003

What Carr's Critics are Saying

"Carr's categorical assertions must be challenged. Information technologies are too important to be pronounced as irrelevant. Such news is prematurely injurious to the health of our economy."[3]
—Paul Strassmann, Executive Advisor, NASA; Former CIO of General Foods, Kraft, Xerox, DoD and NASA

"When IT became over-hyped, we were a little concerned about the promises that were being made during those times. At this stage, in a sense, you could say IT's almost under-hyped ... the most extreme [example] was probably the *Harvard Business Review* of suggesting that railroads and IT had a certain similarity, and now that the tracks have been laid, there was no competitive advantage to be had from having better IT systems."[4]
—Bill Gates, CEO, Microsoft

"Even technology that's a commodity still provides business flexibility."[5]
—Tony Scott, CTO General Motors

"The fundamental point is this. The move to a common infrastructure does not reduce the opportunities for competitive advantage; it increases them."[6]
—Vijay Gurbaxani, Professor, University of California

"[Carr] absolutely misses the point ... information technology puts value into goods and services, which are intellectual goods in one form of another ... As a nation and as a company you either upgrade your IT infrastructure or you won't be competitive."[7]
—Craig Barrett, Chief Executive, Intel Corporation

"Extracting business value from IT requires innovations in business practices. In many respects, we believe Carr attacks a red herring—few people would argue that IT alone provides any significant business value or strategic advantage. Carr's article is dangerous because it endorses the growing view that IT offers only limited potential for strategic differentiation."[8]
—John Seely Brown, Former Chief Scientist, Xerox and John Hagel, Management Consultant and Author

"It is premature to think that IT has reached its plateau. It is as if someone claimed that the telephone reached its strategic plateau when the top 25 companies had access to it. Like the telephone, IT is a network phenomenon. Wal-Mart for example, benefits from their IT investment more as more of their supplier base is IT-enabled."[9]
—Rajiv Gupta, father of e-services (later re-labeled Web services), Chairman and CTO, Confluent Software

"Surely one of the great inanities of 2003 is Harvard Business Review's May 2003 article, "IT Doesn't Matter." From the other coast, we're getting the same message from Larry Ellison [Oracle Corp.], claiming that tech has become mature—only a few big companies will dominate, as in the car industry. And Larry's out to prove his case with M&A silliness. As it turns out, Larry and HBR are half right, and therefore totally wrong."[10]
—George F. Colony, CEO and President, Forrester Research

"Think of IT like the food that comes into a restaurant—yes, the meat and vegetables most restaurants use are commodities that anyone can buy themselves, but what the restaurant does with the food is what really matters."[11]
—Chad Dickerson, CTO of *Infoworld*

"Carr simply misunderstands what information technology is."[12]
—David Kirkpatrick, *Fortune Magazine*

"In no other area is it more important to have a sense of what you *don't* know than it is in IT management. The most dangerous advice to CEOs has come from people who either had no idea of what they didn't know, or from those who pretended to know what they didn't. Couple not knowing what you don't know with fuzzy logic, and you have the makings of Nicholas Carr's article."[13]

—F. Warren McFarlan, Richard L. Nolan, Professors, Harvard Business School

"The use of IT is analogous to innovations in transportation, not power utilities. Common standards like roads and airports exist, but the cars we choose to drive and our methods of travel are based on individual preference. IT utilities will exist, but businesses will derive unique benefits from how they leverage specific technologies. I just think of walking into our living room and telling my kids that we now have a 'TV Utility' and the only channel we get is C-SPAN. I don't think they would consider this a step forward."[14]

— Mark S. Lewis, Executive Vice President,
EMC Corporation

"Our fundamental response to that [article] is: hogwash."[15]
—Steve Ballmer, CEO and President, Microsoft

"The argument in 'IT Doesn't Matter' goes roughly like this: Kidneys don't matter. Kidneys are basically a commodity. Just about everyone has kidneys. There is no evidence that CEOs with superior kidneys are more successful than CEOs with average kidneys. In fact, CEOs who spend more on their kidneys often don't do as well."[16]
—Steven Alter, Professor of Information Systems, University of San Francisco School of Business and Management

IT Doesn't Matter
—Business Processes Do

A Critical Analysis of Nicholas Carr's I.T. Article
in the *Harvard Business Review*[17]

Howard Smith and Peter Fingar

MK

Meghan-Kiffer Press
Tampa, Florida, USA, www.mkpress.com
Advanced Business-Technology Books
for Competitive Advantage

Publisher's Cataloging-in-Publication Data

Smith, Howard.
IT Doesn't Matter—Business Processes Do: A Critical analysis of Nicholas Carr's I.T. Article in the Harvard Business Review / Howard Smith and Peter Fingar, - 1st ed.
    p. cm.
    Includes appendix.
    ISBN 0-929652-35-5

    1. Management 2. Technological innovation. 3. Strategic planning. 4. Management information systems. 5. Information technology. 6. Information resources management. 7. Organizational change. I. Smith, Howard. II. Fingar, Peter. III. Title

HD58.87.S548 2003   2003109327
658.4'063–dc21   CIP

Published by Meghan-Kiffer Press
310 East Fern Street — Suite G
Tampa, FL 33604 USA

Company and product names mentioned herein are the trademarks or registered trademarks of their respective owners.

Meghan-Kiffer books are available at special quantity discounts for corporate education and training use. For more information write Special Sales, Meghan-Kiffer Press, Suite G, 310 East Fern Street, Tampa, Florida 33604 or email sales@mkpress.com

Meghan-Kiffer Press
USA

Printed in the United States of America.   SAN 249-7980
MK Printing 10 9 8 7 6 5 4 3 2 1

This book is dedicated to business leaders who want to go deeper into the provocative ideas asserted in "IT Doesn't Matter," published in the *Harvard Business Review*, May 2003.

IT's not about the last 50 years,
IT's about the next 50 years.

Contents

You've no doubt seen or heard talk of "IT Doesn't Matter" in the May 2003 issue of Harvard Business Review. It's one of those rare pieces of Harvard-speak that will be heard around the world, the likes of which hasn't been seen since HBR published Michael Hammer's "Reengineering Work: Don't Automate, Obliterate!" in 1990. That article triggered the great business reengineering and 'downsizing' wave. As Bob Evans of Information Week reported, "Carr's unshakeable belief leads him to a conclusion that's no doubt provocative ... but also profoundly short sighted and dangerous."[18]

Dangerous Articles

Did Evans rightfully dub Carr's article "dangerous?" Yes, dangerous, for the *interpretations* of Hammer's 1990 article led to great disruption and damage. CEOs across the land waved the article and later the follow-on book, *Reengineering the Corporation,* as a justification for "downsizing," or less euphemistically, "firing people." Indeed, many downsized themselves to the point of anemia. All this was in response to the extreme pain companies felt in the late '80s as globalization was kicking in and Japan dispelled the belief that a business could compete on just one of the three competitive variables: speed to market, better quality, or cost. Indeed Japanese manufacturers were dominating global markets by competing on both cost and quality.

Dangerous? Yes, dangerous, because once again great pain is being felt in the business world—the bursting of the dot-com bubble, trillions sucked out of public financial markets and the uncertainty of global terrorism. While the types of arguments that Carr puts forward are clearly riding the current backlash wave of the irrational IT overspend of the late 1990s, we now have the emergence of an "IT Ice Age," and many CEOs will no doubt wave Carr's article in the air and put IT spending into a deep freeze (cryogenics if they could)—anything to cut costs in today's down-turned economy. Whether intentionally or not, Carr, an independent business writer and consultant, has emerged as the poster-child for those who believe the IT sector is now a sunset industry. As the poster-child, his thesis could be quite handy for CEOs looking to justify downsizing and IT spending freezes. Indeed, following Carr's cost-control and risk-mitigation prescriptions, misguided executives can now more readily justify *downsizing* IT.

Hammer talked of two companies in his article, one of which went out of business before his best-selling book was published three years later. The other company's story was about streamlining 3-way matching of orders, invoices and receiving documents, and that is certainly not a very strategic issue. But worse, his article has been argued to have inflicted damage to companies that didn't look deeper into the underlying issues suggested in the text. It seemed that some companies only wanted to hear sound bites.

"Don't automate, obliterate!" became the clarion call of all those who set out to remove workers, rather than—as Hammer had intended—re-design work processes. The misuse of Hammer's work, and the intent behind his slogan, was partly a backlash against the tendency of some corporations, entranced by new computer systems, to believe that further enhancements in productivity could be gained solely by a redeployment of office-automation systems, rather than the much harder task of serious and significant organizational re-design. Will Carr's article suffer the same fate, and will Carr, like Hammer before him, write in future issues of HBR of how the industry at large misunderstood his intent?

On the other hand, not everyone steers their business based on magazine articles. One such person *not* setting his future on Harvard-speak is Bill Gates who obviously concluded that "Harvard Doesn't Matter," dropped out of Harvard, and well, you know the story. One such company who won't be waving Carr's article in the air to irrationally justify cutting IT costs is GE. Beginning in 2000, as the stunning collapse of the dot-coms and the prevailing economic winds led the lemmings among the brick-and-mortar companies to decimate technology budgets, GE increased IT spending in 2001 by 12 percent, to $3 billion.[19] To GE, IT matters.

Why has GE increased its IT budget in the midst of a major economic downturn? The answer was put in writing in GE's 2002 Key Growth Initiatives, "Digitization is the greatest growth opportunity our company has ever seen." It's a similar story at Silicon Valley poster child, Cisco Systems. Responding to Carr, CIO Brad Boston, states, "Cisco Systems has 1.9 billion reasons to believe IT does matter. That's the amount of money Cisco saved last year thanks to our investments in information technology. I'm referring to the same kinds of information technology that companies around the world use to run their accounting, customer service, e-business, financial management, and nearly every other task. Thanks to our strategic use of information technology, we not only lowered operational costs but also improved customer service and created better workforce intelligence, among countless other benefits. The key to Cisco's strategic use of information technology has been not how much we spend but how we spend it."[20]

Are GE and Cisco talking about the same "IT" as Nicholas Carr? We think not. Words like *IT, computerization, automation, and information* are vague, and subject to as many definitions as the number of people you ask.

The IT World According to Carr

Nicholas G. Carr is an independent writer, consultant and former member of the *Harvard Business Review* editorial staff who penned the article that has stirred much debate in business and technology circles. If you haven't read the article we encourage you to obtain a copy. It can be obtained from HBR or Amazon.com via a link at www.bpm3.com/hbr.

It is important that you read his thesis in full, for it is compelling, yet we are firmly of the opinion that his conclusions are wrong. We form that judgment based on our own research both before and after the publication of Carr's article and on the basis of the content of numerous rebuttals to Carr from around the world, which we have researched and discussed here in order to construct and expand our critical analysis.

His analysis has clearly identified an Achilles' heel in the IT industry, and it is this: Carr argues that technology's potential for differentiating one company from the pack—its strategic potential—inexorably diminishes as it becomes accessible and affordable to all. Thomas Stewart, writing in the introduction to a series of "Letters to the Editor" following publication of Carr's article, states, "The most common misperception [of Carr's ideas] is that the article says that IT is dead and that it will not continue to be a source of dramatic, even transformational change. It doesn't say that. Instead, it says the odds are that the benefits of such changes will inure to whole industries, rather than any one competitor."[21]

Stewart's interpretation of Carr's argument lies at the heart of our analysis also, for we argue here, and in our previous work, that recent changes in IT itself are now able to address the management of a company's unique, differentiated business processes, and do so in a manner that leads to the exact opposite conclusion as Carr's. The benefits of the coming era of *process-oriented* IT will inure to individual companies and will substantially assist them in dominating the value chains they manage. Indeed, the front cover of our previous work, *Business Process Management: The Third Wave,* states "The breakthrough that redefines competitive advantage for the next fifty years." Thus, when Carr's article appeared in a widely distributed journal such as HBR, we felt compelled to respond.

To provide you a preamble of our critique, and so as not to distort in any way what he has written, here is the essence of Carr's thesis in his own words. "I examine the evolution of information technology in business and show that it follows a pattern strikingly similar to earlier technologies like railroads and electric power. For a brief period, as they are being built into the infrastructure of commerce, these 'infrastructural technologies,' as I call them, open opportunities for forward-looking companies to gain sustainable competitive advantages. But as their availability increases and their cost decreases—as they become ubiquitous—they become commodity inputs. From a strategic standpoint, they become invisible; they no longer matter. ... In brief, executives need to shift their attention from IT opportunities to IT risks—from offense to defense."[22]

The following are snippets that we will use to illustrate Carr's specific assertions and upon which we base our analysis in this book. Some will be repeated as this book progresses and we address the issues raised.

"As IT's power and ubiquity have grown, its strategic importance has diminished."

"What makes a resource truly strategic is not ubiquity, but scarcity. You only gain an edge over rivals by having or doing something that they can't have or do. By now, the core functions of IT—data storage, data processing, and data transport—have become available and affordable to all. Their very power and presence have begun to transform them from potentially strategic resources into commodity factors of production."

"[data storage, data processing, and data transport] are becoming costs of doing business that must be paid by all but provide distinction to none."

"IT is best seen as the latest in a series of broadly adopted technologies that have reshaped industry over the past two centuries—from the steam engine and the railroad to the telegraph and the telephone to the electric generator to the internal combustion engine."

"The *buildout* [of infrastructural technology] forces users to adopt technical standards, rendering proprietary systems obsolete. Even the way the [infrastructural] technology is used becomes standardized as best practices come to be widely understood and emulated. Often, in fact, the best practices end up being built into the infrastructure itself. ... Both the technology and its modes of use become, in effect, commoditized."

"IT is also highly replicable. Indeed it is hard to imagine a more perfect commodity than a byte of data—endlessly and perfectly reproducible at virtually no cost. The near-infinite scalability of many IT functions, when combined with technical standardization, dooms most proprietary applications to economic obsolescence. Why write your own application ... when you can buy ready-made, state-of-the-art application for a fraction of the cost?"

And Carr's key recommendations drawn from these assertions, his "New Rules for IT management," are:

1. "Spend less;
2. Follow, don't lead; and
3. Focus on vulnerabilities, not opportunities."

In the May 12, 2003 issue of ComputerWorld, Carr reasserted his fundamental ideas, "… Companies have increasingly bought into the assumption that IT is a strategic resource. As a result, they have brought in CIOs who are conceptual, strategic thinkers about IT. I think there's less of a need for those types of individuals."[23]

Carr is Right—In a Wrong Kind of Way

Carr is absolutely right when he observes that "… most companies can reap significant savings by simply cutting out waste. Personal computers are a good example. Every year, businesses purchase more that 100 million PCs, most of which replace older models. Yet the vast majority of workers who use PCs rely on only a few simple applications—word processing, spreadsheets, e-mail, and Web browsing. Nevertheless, companies continue to roll out across-the-board hardware and software upgrades." And he's right to ask, "Why write your own application for word processing or e-mail?" Carr is also right when he notes that, "companies have been sloppy in their use of IT. That's particularly true with data storage." And he is spot on when he writes that "few companies have done a thorough job of identifying and tempering their vulnerabilities." On the other hand, these observations can relate to *any* company asset and can point to *poor management*, not the relationship between IT and strategic advantage.

From the reactions of Evans, Boston and others, we congratulate Carr on a timely and excellent piece of journalism that has led business people (and those in the tech sector that serve them) to really think! Carr's article is a kind of "State of the Business-IT Union" that reflects the *data-centric* mental models of the past fifty years still used by many to understand IT.

While Carr serves as a lightning rod and shocks people into thinking about IT, after reading his article, we ask business leaders to *think again*. Although Carr's article embodies several "individual truths," his assumptions, premises and conclusions all merit closer examination if, as in the Indian story of the Blind Men and the Elephant, the whole picture of IT and business strategy are to come into focus. For as he says, "Information Technology is a fuzzy term." In his article he defines IT "as denoting the technologies used for processing, storing and transporting information in digital form." By restricting his definition, he looks at only parts of the elephant, and therein lies the grave danger for business leaders who read it and draw conclusions for the whole of IT.

Carr is right about many of the individual points he makes, but is he right about the *right things* when it comes to the role of IT in enabling strategic advantage or his conclusion that IT doesn't matter? The careful reader will demand to know not only where he is right but also what he has omitted—that is, the *full* scope of IT as it relates to competitive advantage. After all, an elephant's tail is not an elephant.

Business Infrastructure	Business Automation	Process Management
• Office environment – email, desktop, portals etc	• Data Processing, automation of existing ways of working	• Business Enabler
• Lowest cost source • Enables business to communicate and share information	• Standardization • Provides audit trail • Supports scaling of business • Reduces head count. • Provides management reporting	• Translates business requirements into reality • Enhances understanding • Provides actionable feedback • Enables differentiation
• Required by all	• Type of business determines need	• How the business develops, delivers and maintains market position

The next 50 years of IT

The last 50 years of IT

Figure 1. The Full Scope of IT Today

Business consultant Bob Lewis wrote his overall assessment of Carr's article, "Sometimes, being right is more misleading than being wrong. ... in [Carr's] view [IT] has become so plentiful and commoditized that it no longer provides anyone with a competitive advantage. He is, of course, right. In a wrong kind of way. ... Yes, if we lived in press-release land, Carr might possibly be correct. We might have reached the point of diminishing returns, and information technology won't provide any further competitive advantage. Failing to invest in IT will, in this world of trade-journal fiction, lead to huge competitive disadvantages, but that's a different story. Except ... it isn't about information technology. It's always about how business gets done. IT is an enabler of *business processes* and practices, not a separate and distinct provider of value."

"Businesses either change or they fail. They adopt new strategies and reconfigure themselves to implement those strategies on a regular basis. They improve their internal processes and practices continuously and change their IT to support the improvements. Even for companies with the most flexible application architectures, adapting them to these business changes is difficult and time-consuming. IT fails and the strategy fails. IT fails and business improvement fails. IT doesn't matter? For this to be true, how you conduct business can't have an impact on your success in the marketplace. So even in the land of press releases, Carr can only be right if strategy doesn't matter, and business processes and practices have reached optimization nirvana ... there are, that is to say, no competitive advantages to be had, except, maybe, for whom has the better advertising."[24] But then, advertising is a commodity, too, leaving us with business process management as *the* central the issue.

Carr's article is a *red herring*, distracting management attention from the crux of IT today. As British American Tobacco's Gillian Taylor[25] explains, "For many years Carr's 'processing, storing and transporting information in digital form,' arguably has been the definition of information technology, or rather 'data processing.' But is this really the case today?"

"Generations of technology development have brought about a world where IT touches each of us every day, in working practices and home life. Of course IT can be deconstructed to the molecular level, but how useful is it to do so? In today's fast-moving business environment, how we put those molecules together becomes critical in supporting competitive differentiation."

"The spark of life for IT in the business environment is the requirement of the business to fulfill corporate strategy. Corporate strategy flexes and changes over time, and requires both people and systems to work together to achieve common goals. In the past, IT has provided the systems part; but the potential for IT has moved on significantly in managing both elements of people and business systems. This orchestration of information manipulation and human contribution is what both the business and IT community refer to as business process management, which is made possible by continuing major advances in IT. The ability to design, execute and optimize processes in an inclusive loop, through the boardroom to IT and back again, means that for the first time, the business and IT can work from the same sheet at all points in the process lifecycle."

Taylor points to that which is conspicuously missing in Carr's analysis (the third column in the figure above): the emergence of a *breakthrough in business automation, a totally new category of information systems* that has little to do with "IT" as most know it today. Nor does it have anything to do with three-letter IT acronyms or with the next "big-bang" killer app.

Instead the new framework for business information systems has to do with the humble, yet MIGHTY, "business process." Carr's argument that companies should "manage costs and risks meticulously" coupled with the headline "IT Doesn't Matter" could easily deflect management attention from this breakthrough in enabling competitive advantage, which in turn, has been made possible by a breakthrough technology that has emerged on the business-IT scene over the past four or five years. Twenty years of computer science[26], three years of standards development[27] and six years of product R&D, have finally yielded new post-Carr-era technologies capable of dealing directly with end-to-end business processes.

Companies are just now beginning to learn how to harness this new strategic capability, linking process management to the balance sheet. The business process management breakthrough represents a tipping point dominated, for the first time since the advent of business computing, by the *business* side of the business-IT equation.

So, if you are a businessperson who understands the business process management revolution,[28] you will no doubt hope that Carr's HBR article does become wildly popular! Following the advice he dispenses, your competitors will, like lemmings, follow the red herring piper right off the cliff and focus their energies into stopping those pesky PC upgrades and otherwise putting IT spending in the deep freeze, wrongly thinking they can gain new competitive advantage by *saving* their way to market dominance!

You will of course know otherwise and continue to invest *appropriately* and *aggressively* in technology-enabled business process management. For, as the research firm, Gartner concludes, "Business process management wins the 'triple crown' of saving money, saving time and adding value. It also spans the business and technological gap to create synergy, with proven results. BPM is delivering both short-term return on investment (ROI) and long-term value (VOI)."[29]

Nine Key Issues

Throughout our critical analysis we cite specific instances of Carr's thesis and conclusions he draws. They cover the following areas:

1. Industrial-Age Versus Information-Age Technology
2. The IT Industry Versus The Business Use of IT
3. Infrastructural Technologies
4. The First Fifty Years of Business and IT
5. "Applications" Versus Business Process Management
6. Grids, Web Services and Computing Utilities
7. The Essence of Web Services
8. Best-Practice and Best-in-Class Business Processes
9. The IT Buildout

What follows is an overview of our conviction that, contrary to his advice, we believe that companies should lead, not follow, in the next phase of IT buildout, focussed as it is on business processes, not just business data. But as we do this critique of Carr's analysis, no one should construe that we are criticising Nicholas Carr, for the debate he has initiated is important, vital even, to the world economy. It is a debate which started a long time ago, even before our book was published, and indeed, as we say in that work "The third wave of business process management was conceived in response to the chaos companies find around them as they position themselves for 21st century competition." What Carr has done, has put the matter firmly on the radar and raised the level of awareness further.

1. Industrial-Age versus Information-Age Technology

The Issue: *Industrial-Age technology doesn't equate with Information-Age technology.*

Carr closes his opening arguments with, "Information technology is best understood as the latest in a series of broadly adopted technologies that have reshaped industry over the past two centuries—from the railroad to the telegraph to the electric generator. For a brief period, as they were being built into the infrastructure of commerce, all these technologies opened opportunities for forward-looking companies to gain real advantages. But as their availability increased and their cost decreased—as they became ubiquitous—they all became commodity inputs. From a strategic standpoint, they became invisible; they no longer mattered. That is exactly what is happening to information technology today, and the implications for corporate IT management are profound."

Here as elsewhere in Carr's article, the industrial-age technologies Carr describes deal with the *physical world*, technologies that amplify and extend the powers of the human body. The steam engine and the electric generator provide energy to amplify man's muscles, the railroad amplifies man's legs and the telephone amplifies and extends the human voice. In stark contrast, a mark of the human kind is the ability to manipulate information outside the human body, and *information automation* should not be compared to *mechanization* in the physical world.

In the physical world, as Carr explains, *scarcity* may be the basis for sustainable competitive advantage, but not in the worlds of the human mind where innovation and creativity are unbounded resources. Let's not petition to close the Patent office by extrapolating on such scarcity-versus-commodity logic in the intangible world of human creation and innovation.

Industry luminary and veteran CIO Paul Strassmann

elaborates, "There is not a shred of evidence that IT developments have reached a plateau as did innovations in industrial-age machinery. Physical mechanics impose limits on the size and performance of locomotives, turbines, airplanes, refrigerators and trucks; there are no such confinements to information technologies, as far as we can tell. Software can endow computing devices with unrestricted variability in features and function. The capability of a software-enriched global network has no boundaries."[30]

EMC's Executive Vice President Mark Lewis agrees, "Carr's historical analogies to other infrastructure technologies are not convincing. Information technology has infinite and constantly expanding functionality."[31] As Intel chief executive Craig Barrett reported in the Guardian newspaper, "unlike most industrial technologies that make or move materials, IT is the vehicle by which you turn ideas and content into intellectual property products"[32]—whether that's Intel's next chip, Boeing's next plane or drugs tailored to individual DNA. Chief information officer at the London Stock Exchange, David Lester, was reported as heading an IT function that is "responsible for nearly 50% of business because the exchange sells information and prices. Spending a third of the company budget on IT is unusual—but so is halving the cost and time of developing new products."[33]

2. The IT Industry versus The Business Use of IT

The Issue: Carr's article is about technology as a business (the IT Industry), not the business use of technology for competitive advantage

The second critical flaw is that Carr wrongly intermixes *technology as a business* (something done by a technology provider company, an IT vendor) with a business that *uses* information technology to conduct business. By speaking of a *buildout* of IT infrastructure technology, he argues that best practices are automatically embedded in the infrastructure and all who use it become commoditized.

That's like saying all who use the builtout telephone

systems of today have nothing unique to say, or all who use the builtout alphabet are reduced to commodities in their writing. We conclude that Carr is really writing about commoditization in the IT industry, *not* the use of IT for strategic advantage where commoditized infrastructure technologies can exponentially multiply, not constrict, an individual company's opportunities for building and strengthening relationships with customers, suppliers and trading partners.

University of California professor Vijay Gurbaxani explains, "The fundamental point is this. The move to a common infrastructure does not reduce the opportunities for competitive advantage; it increases them."[34]

Convergent Strategies' CEO, David Ticoll, clarifies, "Instead of information technology, think about information 'deployment' (how you create, capture, deliver, and use information in your business). To say that information deployment will be fully commoditized in the near future is like saying innovation itself will be commoditized."[35]

The problem is that "Information Technology," as defined by Carr, is a fuzzy (his word), ill-defined, term, and he looks at it from the technology provider's perspective—but then goes on to incorrectly render specific conclusions from the technology consumer's perspective.

Paul Chwelos, professor at University of British Columbia and a specialist in the relationship between productivity and IT spending, agrees, stating "Comparing IT to the electrical grid is a seductive argument in that it holds an element of truth."[36] As we shall show however, information technology does not obey the laws of railroads and therefore conclusions based on these analogies must, at least, be highly suspect.

3. Infrastructural Technologies

The Issue: *Infrastructural technologies provide their business users opportunities for competitive advantage when they approach critical mass, not early in their development.*

Carr writes, "As with earlier infrastructural technologies, IT provided forward-looking companies many opportunities for competitive advantage early in its buildout, when it could be owned like a proprietary technology. A classic example is American Hospital Supply. A leading distributor of medical supplies, AHS, introduced in 1976 an innovative system called ASAP that enabled hospitals to order goods electronically. ... By the dawn of the 1990s, after AHS merged with Baxter Travenol to form Baxter International, the company's senior executives had come to view ASAP as 'a millstone around their necks,' according to a Harvard Business School case study."

AHS didn't own the proprietary data communication technology (the IBM 1001 dataphone) it used to enable hospitals to order goods electronically, it was just an early adopter. Back then (pre-Internet) data communication technology was indeed proprietary, buggy and expensive, off putting to others until the technology crossed the chasm, stabilized, and became mainstream. What AHS owned was a primitive ordering system that, although pretty bad according to today's standards, brought them temporary advantage by being a pioneer in using the then emerging data communications technology.

What the AHS story proves is that it's not the infrastructural technology, but the quality of the business process that's delivered over the technology that counts! Even really bad business processes can turn a buck when only proprietary technology is available to get at them, and your competitor is too conservative to make the move or your customers are unwilling to adopt more than one expensive and awkward technology solution. Put those same bad business processes in the light of day when the infrastructural technologies cross the chasm and go mainstream, and you too would throw them out, ASAP. Baxter did this when it went to its ASAP*Express EDI system, and then to its Internet-based OnCall system.

In contrast, American Airlines Sabre was an early adopter of proprietary data communication technology that gave travel agents great advantage even though they had to memorize codes and awkward keystrokes to use the system. But the reservation processes embodied in Sabre were so good that when an easy-to-use Web front end was built, Travelocity became a dominant player in the online reservation business. Infrastructural technology has nothing whatsoever to do with the quality or uniqueness of the business process, except, perhaps to expose bad business processes for all to see as the infrastructure goes mainstream. If proof is needed, go talk to companies that had poor back-office processes exposed when they were forced to go on-line (ill advisedly and prematurely) to provide self-service Web sites in order to compete with companies that had better processes amplified by on-line strategies.

Companies that *provide* infrastructural technologies, e.g. companies in the IT and telecommunications industries, have many opportunities for competitive advantage early in their life, when the technology's buildout has only just begun and the capability provided by the infrastructure can be owned like a proprietary technology.

For companies that *consume* those technologies in their business, infrastructural technologies provide opportunities for competitive advantage when they approach critical mass, not early in their development. Even then, this is only the case *if* they can compete with distinctive business processes that flow through the infrastructure to produce compelling value for their customers.

The Internet, which has been around since the late 1960's, once provided proprietary advantage to the Department of Defense's Advanced Research Projects Agency (DARPA) and the research universities that developed and used it. Later telecommunications companies adopting packet-switching technologies created their own proprietary, private internets. It was only when the non-proprietary Internet and the World Wide Web emerged that the tsunami of the Internet's opportunities for competitive advantage reached the business world. Even then, it was still the fundamentals of competitive advantage—distinctiveness and fit—that could be *amplified* by the technology when it reached critical mass.

Although just about any company can now have access to the Internet, only those that can deliver business processes with compelling value derive and sustain business advantage. Hence, driven by the rise of open standards such as Internet-based Web services, we now observe a resurgence of interest in process management and in technologies that can support the differentiated processes of companies. Their value is amplified by the network effect across companies' value chains.

4. The First Fifty Years of Business and IT

The Issue: *Carr's article is about the beginning of the end of the first fifty years of business and IT, not the end of the beginning of the second fifty years*

With the advent of the first commercial computer, the Univac II in 1952, what Carr today calls IT was then called "tabulating." With the advent of the IBM 360 mainframe in 1964, IT was called "data processing." Perhaps IT replaced the moniker EDP when companies needed to take charge of and manage the growing telecommunications and data network resources they began buying (EDP + telecommunications resources = IT). The data processing department was charged to take on responsibility for the sophisticated telephone PBX systems, and companies began using the new term "IT," since more than data processing alone was involved. Why then was the telephone system handed over to data processing staff? The stuff was technical and mechanical and the best expertise in a company for such matters was indeed the data processing department. Thus, IT was born. Regardless of when or why the name switch took place, business automation for the past fifty years was all about *data*. Accordingly, Carr's misperception is that, "the core functions of IT [are] *data* storage, *data* processing, and *data* transport."

While such a perception may be appropriate for the past, starting four or five years ago and for the years ahead, the core functions of IT are *business process* storage, *business process* processing, and *business process* transport—the unification of computing and communication. As we will explain, all is changed as *data processing* gives way to *process processing*, and business leaders learn that they can finally execute strategy innovations using agile, unique, proprietary (to them) and technology-enabled business processes that *harness* commoditized infrastructural transport and processing technologies. It is indeed the very commoditized channels that present profound growth opportunities for companies that use them to extend their distinctive business processes to the smallest of trading partners and the most remote customers across the globe.

The commoditized IT standards that Carr links to the theme "IT Doesn't Matter" are in fact precisely those that create the opportunity to link companies more easily and cost effectively with their trading partners, suppliers and customers. Such possibilities open up, not close down, opportunities to apply business insight and creativity in order to compete. Industry leaders in many sectors are building these powerful ecosystems in order to compete head-on, value-chain against value-chain. Such competitive strategies are not *embedded* in the IT infrastructure and available to competitors. Quite the contrary, they are *enabled* by the infrastructure.

5. Applications versus Business Process Management

The Issue: *Carr's article is about functional applications, not end-to-end business process management, which is the real frontier for business and IT*

A central problem in Carr's premises is his use of the term "application" when he writes, "IT is also highly replicable. Indeed it is hard to imagine a more perfect commodity than a byte of data—endlessly and perfectly reproducible at virtually no cost. The near-infinite scalability of many IT functions, when combined with technical standardization, dooms most proprietary applications to economic obsolescence. Why write your own application ... for supply chain management when you can a buy ready-made, state-of-the-art application for a fraction of the cost?"

Today's companies are less focused on applications than

they are on tying applications together internally and with business partners to automate end-to-end business processes. But even within the realm of applications as Carr describes them, standard IT solution packages don't dictate the *processes* running on them, that's determined by the businesses that use the packages. Tailoring today's packaged enterprise applications is a common, though tedious, means of making an otherwise packaged solution function as, what Carr calls, a "proprietary application." This is old hat. Paul Strassmann elaborates, "Even the most tightly controlled generic application suite (SAP's enterprise resource planning application) can deliver completely different results for look-alike firms."[37] Even so, the business issues in IT go well beyond the issues of computer applications and on to the digitization of business processes themselves—a trend that's been well underway for the last few years.

For the past fifty years, business "applications" have been all about *functional* automation. Today, most of a company's business processes are trapped inside software that automates one specialized, and usually inward-focused, back-office business function and its activities, e.g., the inventory system or the order entry application. Companies began to use IT tools such as enterprise application integration (EAI) to tap the specific business processes trapped in functional applications, which were often buried in ERP suites, and integrate them into *end-to-end business processes* that bring *ultimate value to customers*. To do this, companies had to integrate their trading partners' functional applications because many companies (suppliers, suppliers' suppliers, etc.) are involved in the value chains that touch the ultimate customer.

AMR Research describes a completely new class of business automation systems, "systems of process" that sit on top of legacy applications that currently, and will continue to, serve as "systems of record." The new focus of business automation is on systems of process, those systems that support a company's own end-to-end business processes.

Carr's article misses the existence of the end-to-end business process and refers instead to functional applications when he speaks of best practices and commoditization. It's just fine if functional applications and off-the-shelf components become best practice, for that's not what counts in creating distinction and strategic advantage—the stuff of distinctive, end-to-end business processes that span the value chain, creating end-to-end processes that matter to customers.

The paradigm shift from *applications* to *business processes* in the world of business automation can be confirmed by observing that today every major IT vendor now has business process management (BPM) at the top of its technology stack and that new BPM technology start-ups are emerging, as Oracle Corporation was once a start up during the rise of relational data systems. For some application developers, business process management systems are emerging as the next strategic platform, replacing the database of the last decades. This shift goes all the way down to the theoretical underpinnings of IT, the mathematics.

Relational algebra underpins database management systems and lambda calculus does the same for computer programming. Neither provides the required foundation for dealing with the messy dynamics of business processes. A new math and a new computer science were needed and have indeed been adopted by pioneers in the IT industry. The math is pi-calculus and it underpins the computer science of distributed mobile processes. Both of these developments are not new. They are based on decades of work by people like Cambridge professor Robin Milner, winner of the ACM Turing Award, the Nobel Prize equivalent for computer science. Over the past four or five years, this established body of computer science has been repurposed from scientific uses to commercial business uses and serves as the basis of new information systems capable of handling the dynamics of business processes. Business process management systems can, for the first time in the history of business automation, let companies deal directly with business processes: their discovery, design, deployment, change and optimization.

That is why we are only at the beginning of any sort of IT buildout. We know how to do record keeping with computers, but are only beginning to learn to master business processes, the entity that spans applications, systems, departments and companies; and the entity that will ultimately replace functional applications as we know them today.

Business process pioneer, Michael Hammer, observes that companies know how to do a lot of things that can be understood as processes, such as finding new customers, developing new products and opening new plants. On the other hand, converting general process descriptions into executable processes is difficult for many companies because it is not something in which they have a lot of experience. Improving processes to better serve current customers; using strong processes to enter new markets; expanding processes to provide additional services; taking a process in which you excel and providing it as a service to other companies; adapting processes in which you excel to the creation and delivery of other goods or services; creating new processes to deliver new goods or services—these are activities in which no one has much practical experience. Why? Their cost and complexity were prohibitive in the age of reengineering. This is why mastering the new breakthrough BPM methods and systems changes the calculus for gaining strategic advantage, and those who succeed can look forward to competing during the *next* fifty years of business and IT.

6. Grids, Web Services and Computing Utilities

The Issue: *Grids, Web services and computing utilities don't equate to generic applications—that logic simply doesn't compute*

Nascent Web services aren't about a few IT providers creating Orwellian grids and commoditizing the world with massive best-practices *utilities*. Again, Carr's discussion of commoditization applies to technology vendors slugging it out in a fight to find new ways to deliver computing power. According to Carr, "The arrival of the Internet has accelerated the commoditization of IT by providing a perfect delivery channel for generic applica-

tions. More and more companies will fulfill their IT requirements simply by purchasing fee-based 'Web services' from third
parties—similar to the way we buy electric power and telecommunications. Most major technology vendors, from Microsoft to
IBM, are trying to position themselves as IT utilities, companies
that will control the provision of a diverse range of business applications over what is now called, tellingly, 'the grid.' Again, the
upshot is ever greater homogenization of IT capabilities, as more
and more companies replace customized applications with
generic ones."

Carr's arguments are similar to the invalid tautology: all cats
are mammals; all tigers are mammals, therefore all cats are tigers.
His argument can be easily construed as: grid computing is an
Internet-enabled technology; Web services is an Internet-enabled
technology, therefore the grid is Web services, and more and
more companies will therefore replace customized applications
with generic ones. Huh?

While there was no Microsoft in the 1960s, IBM, GTE and
others worked long and hard to create the computer utility
where dial-up timesharing provided the same services that Carr
describes. Even though, for a short period of time, the new IT
capabilities were provided via time sharing to students and aca-
demic researchers who otherwise wouldn't have been able to
gain mainframe access, most corporations did not use it for their
business computing. In fact, IT industry trends point to the exact opposite need. The capacities of computers are increasing
while their costs are decreasing. Computers are getting smaller
while their capabilities are expanding. There are more specialized
and dedicated computing devices, not fewer and more general
purpose shared devices.

Who needs a utility via a grid when a multiple-processor,
low cost Unix server (or even a cluster of ultra low cost PCs
running open source operating systems such as Linux) can deliver comparable performance? Take into account the attendant
complexities of service level agreements and multi-user resource
management for computer utilities, when compared with the

benefits of ownership and control, particularly in light of global cyber-terrorism, and the case has not been made for the grid. In short, Carr's 'grid world'—and consequently his grid-based, ever greater homogenization of IT capabilities—just may never happen. While some forms of utility computing might become successful, they will not be of the kind that will cause companies to replace customized applications with generic ones.

While Web services can be delivered over the grid if it actually does become a commercial success, grid computing isn't predicated on Web services. A quick visit to *www.whatis.com* can help define the meaning of such technologies, "Grid computing (or the use of a *computational grid*) is applying the resources of many computers in a network to a single problem at the same time—usually to a scientific or technical problem that requires a great number of computer processing cycles or access to large amounts of data." One of the leading companies that wants to provide grid resources in the commercial marketplace, IBM, provides another clear definition, "Grid computing enables the virtualization of distributed computing and data resources such as processing, network bandwidth and storage capacity to create a single system image, granting users and applications seamless access to vast IT capabilities."[38] Neither site mentions Web services.

The grid is really all about the latest evolution of more familiar technologies: distributed computing; the Internet; peer-to-peer; and an autonomic, self-managing computing model. What has this got to do with Web services and companies replacing customized applications with generic ones? Nothing!

If the grid helps companies rid themselves of having to acquire specialized hardware to gain access to computing power, wonderful. Commoditize the heck out of that idea, for with the headaches and complexity out of the way, companies can free up scarce resources and use the grid's commoditized infrastructure, not to diminish the opportunities for competitive advantage, but to increase them. Long live the grid and utility computing, if it succeeds where the 1960s's timesharing didn't. However, buying raw computer power in a manner similar to the way we buy electric power and telecommunications has nothing to do with commoditizing how the utility is used, any more than saying that all who bought IBM mainframes or Intel or Sun servers replaced custom applications with generic ones.

The IT-enabled information society will be driven by visionary companies that see possibilities where others do not and which exploit the low cost, standards-based, plug and play, interconnect-able, networked commodity components to build infrastructures never even predicted.

Indeed, Carr admits this possibility, "This war for scale, combined with the continuing transformation of IT into a commodity, will lead to the further consolidation of many sectors of the IT industry. The winners will do very well; the losers will be gone." Here Carr is referring, once again, to the IT industry itself, but today, more than ever, IT does not exist in a vacuum, isolated from other economic activity.

Take just one example, Visa International and its network, (perhaps we should say "grid") which it based on a precise definition of its business practices and processes and which it enabled by IT. Visa now links in excess of 20,000 financial institutions, 14 million merchants, and 600 million consumers in 220 countries. It is reasonable to expect that it will not be the IT industry that creates the next financial services innovation that will transform our lives. We can, however, be equally sure that IT will matter and must play a major role in making tomorrow's innovations happen.

7. The Essence of Web Services

The Issue: *Carr's references to Web services miss the Essence of Web services technologies*

As we just discussed, Web services are not about grids and utilities. Web services emerged as an answer to the very real technical wall companies hit when they tried to extend application integration outside their own companies to include their trading partners in end-to-end business processes. Web services technology is actually a non-proprietary form of EAI that works natively over the Internet for business-to-business application integration or B2Bi. EAI is proprietary and expensive—it consumes huge portions of the typical IT budget, which itself is a huge component of overall business expense (Carr cites estimates of up to 50% of capital expenditures at the end of the 1990s will be for IT.)[39] Web services do for business-to-business integration what the World Wide Web did for business-to-consumer interactions—they make it easy, inexpensive and ubiquitous. Initially, however, Web services will do little more than lower application integration costs and provide a standard application-programming interface (API) for distributed software components and services. While this is significant to IT developers and IT departments looking to divert every penny of their budget from nugatory to value-added work, this is hardly significant when set against the grand sweep of history that Carr describes using railroad analogies.

But Carr misses an even more important point regarding Web services. As we discussed above, the whole point of integrating applications, internally or externally with trading partners, is to build distinctive, end-to-end business processes that provide unique and compelling value to customers. While companies will use publicly available *commodity* Web services found in digital "Yellow Pages" on the Net (technically speaking, public UDDI registries) just as they use packaged applications today, this is a decision they must make in an informed manner, realizing that the same services are available to competitors. The issues of commodity Web services, such as getting a weather forecast or an exchange rate or a payroll service, are much the same as those best-in-class versus best-of-breed business processes discussed below. On the other hand, companies will also use *private*, carefully controlled and uniquely designed Web services to inexpensively integrate their information systems with their suppliers and trading partners, thus using IT to enable closer links in their value chain. For example, when Home Depot and GE decided to sell GE's major appliances through Home

Depot's retail outlets with GE providing delivery, financing and service, the information systems of the two companies could be knitted together for this strategic business initiative (creating end-to-end business processes) quickly and inexpensively using Web services. Does that mean Home Depot's or GE's applications become commodities open to competitors to buy as commoditized, fee-based Web services? Not on your life. Does this mean the newly integrated process can be optimized in the future? Not without BPM.

Today, both forward-thinking businesses and IT industry players have come to recognize the need to deal directly with the business process instead of application integration as the basis for going forward. Application integration is a technical construct using the semantics of computers, specifically the application program interface or API. Business processes need semantics of their own, not yet more technical semantics if companies are to be able to move the business process center stage in the world of business automation. So, when you get right down to it, even *Web Services Don't Matter—Business Processes Do.*

As Don Tapscott said, "If you abandon the power of IT in enabling you to innovate new business models, then punishment will be swift. You can be a laggard for a while, but then you eventually get blown away by companies with better cost structures, that can *orchestrate* capability better, that have more innovative business strategies and so on."[40] Web services are a connection technology, a technical tool that simplifies the technologists' tasks of connecting software components of disparate functional applications. BPM is a businessperson's tool that simplifies the orchestration of unique business capabilities so that innovative strategies can be executed. Is Web services technology about commoditizing business applications for all to share? Not in your lifetime.

Firms do not and will not expose services on the Internet, hoping partners might use them. Rather, they will explicitly build business models using business processes, and then use Web services to assist with the needed software component "connections" and technical integration.

Web services are needed in the technology stack, but they should be invisible (not matter) to business users of information systems. We already have enough API speak. What we need is more business-process speak so that we can manage dynamic business processes without going back to the technical plumbing.

Paul Andrews also urges us to stay realistic when talking about Web services. "The computer business has always found a way out of a slump. Graphical user interfaces, faster chipsets, the Internet, the Web—all gave juice to the sector right when it started to look as if it had peaked. The next transformative breakthrough, Web services, is just around the corner"[41] he says, pointing to the fact that Web services is as much marketing as it is technology, not something upon which to base decisions about the strategic significance, or otherwise, of IT. Indeed, some tech vendors are already using the Web services marketing moniker to refer to a host of new technologies that have nothing to do with the original Web services technologies. Fundamentally, Web services are the next step in what's technically known as service-oriented application architecture, a movement that began with object-orientation in the 1960s. They are certainly not a new kind of technology that portends application commoditization.

Thomas Davenport astutely warns us about the danger of IT industry monikers in his new book *What's the Big Idea?*, in which he says of knowledge management, "One issue was that too many people—particularly IT vendors—conflated the use of knowledge technologies with the successful management of knowledge. Sometimes this was done in rather obvious ways. One of us, for example, remembers speaking at a KM conference, each attendee's seat was graced with a new publication, *KM World*. How nice, we thought—KM now has it own little newspaper. On examination, however, we discovered that the paper was chock-full of press releases from imaging and document management technology vendors, with only a thin veneer of KM articles on the front page. Only the previous week it had been known as *Imaging World*."[42] Similarly, executives must take care to distinguish between the use of Web services technologies and the management of business processes.

Application integration (with or without Web Services) isn't just a technical issue when one considers the business reasons that drive the need for integration. Ajit Kapoor of Lockheed Martin looks at the human side, "We in our corporations have been accustomed to running our own profit centers and the idea of building common systems, though intellectually enticing, is pragmatically contrary to the human desire to be compensated for results. While we can discuss the complex issues ad-infinitum, the reason can never be deduced to a simple commodity like the nature of information technology (note information technology is different from just technology). Actually, this is the crux of the problem, while we have advanced from the industrial age where cost was the primary mover, our entrance into the information age still carries over our paradigm of working in the industrial age mode."

"I truly believe that the relationship between the CIO and CEO has been that of a 'trophy wife.' Never in my 35 year business career have I seen the CIO being consulted prior to any merger or any acquisition—it's usually after the fact when, for example, the two e-mail systems cannot interoperate. The post merger cost to make systems work together may indeed have contributed to the subconscious feeling of disdain for IT and its value."

"Lately at Lockheed Martin, IT has been given the right visibility from senior management where the relationship of the CIO and CEO is beginning to be comparable to that enjoyed by the CFO in the past. I feel good about the potential of IT in adding strategic value to our business and am certainly not looking forward to explaining to our management the misconception in Mr. Carr's article. Our most recent strategic plan calls for an evolution toward a service-oriented architecture based on the promise of delivering IT services built upon BPM technology where business users create services they need without relying on an IT person to come and scope the project with deliverables in 18 months. Now I may have exaggerated a bit, but you get the point. The service-oriented architecture with BPM is the first time in IT history where the control will be in the hands of users and not IT. But IT has, and will have, a critical role in delivering this paradigm."[43]

8. Best-Practice and Best-in-Class Business Processes

The Issue: *Best-Practice and Best-in-Class business processes are not the same, and companies need both to compete effectively*

Best practices aren't the only practices, as Carr implies, "the opportunities for IT-based advantages are already dwindling. Best practices are now quickly built into software or otherwise replicated." As we showed in our discussion of public and private uses of Web services, companies don't and won't compete by exposing public Web services for all comers. Nor will they compete by using industry best practices as *the* source of competitive advantage, for best practices are necessary and beneficial, but not sufficient. It's only the core competencies embedded into unique business practices that count. For example, Amazon has proprietary, best-in-class business processes so compelling that it provides them to Target, Borders and other brick and mortar giants—but also uses best practice processes such as EDI for ordering from book wholesalers, e.g. Ingram, and EFT best practices for electronically paying its associates and vendors.

Carr never mentions that there's anything else besides best practice, or that companies need both best practices and differentiating, best-in-class, business processes. As a business, I want a best-practice commodity payroll system because I don't compete in my industry based on how uniquely I pay my employees! I might even use Web services to integrate my IT systems with that payroll system. But just don't touch my patented, best-in-class 1-click ordering process, might say Jeff Bezos, CEO at Amazon. The next phase of IT development is being applied to the management of unique, company-differentiated business processes, the very ones that companies use to dominate their markets.

Companies like Wal-Mart have already applied IT for strategic advantage, not by using components that are different from other companies, but by *how* these components are used to support *differentiated business processes.* Does it matter to Wal-Mart whether EDI components of their IT infrastructure are available to competitors? Not in the least. Does it matter to Wal-Mart that EDI components may have become "commodities?" Not in the least. In fact, contrary to Carr's analysis, IT components are, today, increasingly flexible, configurable and able to be applied by companies using highly *differentiated* strategies brought to life with their technology-enabled business processes.

As the IT debate initiated by Carr continues to rage in the media, numerous business process case studies have come to light. To varying degrees they illustrate how companies actually think about business processes, as contrasted by how the IT industry, and particularly packaged software suppliers, understand them. Writer Mark Anderson uncovered a modest but compelling case study in Ottawa, Lee Valley Tools, a high-end tool manufacturer, retailer and catalogue pioneer.

Anderson reported Lee Valley Tools' "business model is one of vertical integration, from R&D, through manufacturing, marketing and sales." President Robin Lee eloquently put the case for process when he said, "IT is part of that [vertical integration], and provides us with tremendous competitive advantage. ... We're not going to write our own word processor or spreadsheet. We'll buy those. But when it comes to core business processes, you either design them yourself, or you allow someone else to decide how your business is going to run. If you don't have control over the IT, you don't have control over your business. We started with an off-the-shelf software package, and then heavily modified it using the case development tool, tailoring virtually every aspect of the package to how we do business. It's absolutely critical. If you just buy off-the-shelf, you can't expect to be better than anyone else. The most you can hope for is to be as good as everyone else, and that's not setting the bar very high."[44]

Anderson concludes that at Lee Valley Tools "IT is integral to and inseparable from the overall competitive strategy. Its value resides not in commoditized hardware and software packages, or even in custom-built applications, but in a staff of IT professionals with an intimate understanding of the underlying business, and who use technology to support it in innovative and organic ways." "It's no longer a question of processor speeds or disks, of collecting and storing data in the most efficient manner," says Lee. "The dog's already caught that car. The question now is what you do with it, and that comes down to an IT staff who know your policies, your methods of operation, what makes you distinct. That's something that can't be commoditized."[45]

In some of his comments Carr appears to admit that a limited form of differentiation using technology is possible. *The New York Times* reported him saying, "My point is that the layer of technology that is customizable, and therefore can give a company a competitive advantage, is getting thinner and thinner ... And technology-based competitive gains won't last as long in the future. I still think my conclusions are true."[46]

In fact, the exact opposite is the case. The latest breakthroughs in computing increase, not decrease, a firms ability to imprint their own business processes upon IT infrastructure. ERP vendors such as SAP and others are scurrying to turn monolithic applications (the ones that do have a thin layer of customization) into fine grained component libraries and adding process management systems to allow their customers to build new processes within days or weeks, not months or years. For ERP vendors, it is now untenable for companies to wait months or years for new IT systems as they were forced to do in the past. BPM has changed their world. Further, the BPM breakthrough goes all the way down to the technical plumbing, transforming that thin layer of customization into a foundation for changeability. While some packaged application vendors may seek to paint over the cracks, the BPM cat is out of the bag, and there is no turning back.

The trend toward business process management has gained tremendous momentum. It is allowing companies to further differentiate their use of IT and gain lifecycle control over all processes. BPM will be used both to differentiate (best-in-class), and to standardize (best-practice). For example, when it comes to compliance with the Sarbanes-Oxley Act, or other regulations, companies, not understanding the process management breakthrough, may seek best practice processes built into new software so that they can, as a peer-group, demonstrate that they are enabling appropriate degrees of transparency and can be held accountable. But what about retrofitting compliance processes to existing systems, for companies have millions of dollars invested in millions of lines of existing code? How can compliance processes be added to legacy systems? Companies will want to provide an overlay of transparent processes over existing systems in order to avoid expensive armies of people being called to the task using only manual methods, tying up valuable resources— and they will want to adjust processes on an ongoing basis.

Quite aside from meeting legal requirements that are mandatory in all business sectors, financial services providers may be able to use regulatory compliance itself as a source of competitive differentiation as long as it can be explained to consumers of financial products. If financial services providers are to continue to persuade investors to part with hard-won funds, the coming battleground may be over trust, not rates. Firms will want to demonstrate providence by developing transparent processes that include all stakeholders as participants: regulators; accountants; insurers and consumers. A similar approach could be equally important in the corporate financial markets.

The complexity and sophistication of such collaborative business-to-business and business-to-consumer processes will be completely dependent upon IT. Process management systems will be a key determinant of a company's ability to provide such processes economically. The creative application of process technologies to financial management will be a critical differentiator among financial institutions. Far from agreeing with Carr that "there will be less need for those types of individuals," referring to CIOs that can think creatively, it will be the whole CxO team's creative application of IT that will be the critical differentiator in the era of process management. The use of IT-enabled BPM to create (and subsequently optimize) processes will be the deciding factor between those financial institutions that grow market share and those that do not. The same will be true in other highly competitive markets.

9. The IT Buildout

The Issue: *There are many signs that the IT buildout is not closer to its end than its beginning.*

Carr argues that "… there are many signs that the IT buildout is much closer to its end than its beginning. First, IT's power is outstripping most of the business needs it fulfills. Second, the price of essential IT functionality has dropped to the point where it is more or less affordable to all. Third, the capacity of the universal distribution network (the Internet) has caught up with demand—indeed, we already have considerably more fiber-optic capacity than we need. Fourth, IT vendors are rushing to position themselves as commodity suppliers or even as utilities. Finally, and most definitely, the investment bubble has burst, which historically has been a clear signal that an infrastructional technology is reaching the end of its buildout. A few companies may still be able to wrest advantages from highly specialized applications that don't offer strong economic incentives for replication, but those firms will be the exceptions that prove the rule."

Overall, Carr is once again writing about the IT industry, not the businesses that consume the infrastructural technologies that the IT industry provides—he is mixing apples and oranges.

IT's Power is Not Outstripping Business Needs

First, IT's power is not outstripping most of the business

needs it can fulfill, it is only beginning to fulfill the true requirements that companies have to create and sustain competitive
advantage. Most IT users report considerable difficulty with IT
systems, and the IT industry has yet to imbue technology with
what W. Brian Arthur, Citibank Professor at the Santa Fe Institute calls the "1001 sub-technologies, arrangements and architectures that adapt us to new technologies and them to us. Their
arrival takes time."[47]

Arthur, whose research interests focus on the economics of
the high technology sector, defines the build-out period as one
that is dependent upon all the sub-inventions that bring the new
possibilities into full use, the possibilities beyond just better,
faster, and cheaper. These discrete sub-inventions are the very
commodity components that Carr rails against. Creating these
use-of-IT perfections at the intersection with our lives, both at
home and at work, will be one of the determining factors between successful and unsuccessful uses of IT, for we are
nowhere near the *amenity* buildout.

Amenity? Arthur explains, "... it is not sufficient that businesses and people adapt to a new cluster of technology. The real
gains come when the new technology adapts to them. The notion that a technology needs to adapt to its users seems obvious
enough, but is heavily underestimated. People will not use a
technology that doesn't work properly. They will shun anything
awkward or untrustworthy or just plain difficult to use. Making
the technology better, faster, cheaper is only part of what's
needed. A new technology is used when it is more convenient,
easier and reliable. For widespread use, a technology must
provide, in a word, amenity."

Just take the Internet itself as an example. As an "infrastructural technology," the Internet has been around since the
late 1960s. Grandma never used the stuff back then because if
you had asked her to use *gopher, ftp and telnet* to shop on the Internet—never mind. But give her the point-and-click World Wide
Web and watch out—it's so easy and so intuitive, you just might
have to cancel her credit card privileges. That's amenity,

something you just don't get in the early stages of infrastructural technologies.

While data-centric uses of IT have taken fifty years to commoditize most back-office record keeping applications (payrolls, inventory management, and so on), we don't need more of the "Old IT," (paraphrasing U.S. Secretary of Defense Donald Rumsfield), we need a *change in kind, of the business-process kind.* IT's power has only just begun fulfilling the pressing business needs for amenity in business process management.

Business processes—the dynamic, expanding, contracting, changing activities of the business—are not so stable or predictable as data and back-office record keeping. In fact, they are extremely messy. Because they are so dynamic and such an overwhelming challenge to computerize, business processes have in the past been second-class citizens in the world of IT, limiting that which has been automated and improved. Only the most basic, back-office business processes are incorporated into the majority of today's IT systems. By contrast, and for exactly the same messy reasons, business processes of all shapes and sizes are the focus of management attention today. For "as consumers and workers, both online and offline, each of us is enveloped by a myriad of business processes—the intricate, dynamic, ever-changing manifestations of the economic activity of companies. Whether we are disinterested, or actively engaged, in these processes, in large part determines the wealth of those who weave them."[48] Companies can only wish that its IT power could outstrip the true business needs it wants to fulfill with business process management to delight customers and partners at all points in the value chain.

When the Price of IT Functionality Drops, That's a Good Thing

Second, as Carr states, "the price of essential IT functionality has dropped to the point where it is more or less affordable to all." Contrary to Carr's conclusions, this correct observation actually opens up a whole new world of opportunity for gaining strategic advantage, for we live in a global economy. Small and medium-size enterprises make up the backbone of the global economy, and as such they are the backbone of most value chains.

According to the Small Business Administration, of the 5.6 million firms in the U.S., a mere 16,378 employ more than 500 workers. Approximately 5.5 million firms employ fewer than 100, while approximately 5 million employ fewer than 20. The next frontier of IT is the little guy, who may never use more than a Web browser and a spreadsheet—in Columbus, Ohio and Durban, South Africa; Shanghai, China; Peoria, Illinois; and Bangalore, India.

Small enterprises are important because they are the weak links in the mission-critical value chains of their larger partners. While industry leaders such as Wal-Mart and GE may be able to make large investments in real-time, automated and auditable connectivity infrastructure, the mom-and-pop shop cannot. However, the burden of that broken link does not rest solely on the mom-and-pop shop, but on the Wal-Marts as well. Every corner of Wal-Mart's extended enterprise that is not fully connected and coordinated subtracts substantially from its bottom line due to the higher costs of manual intervention, slower service and human error.

Wal-Mart is not only interested in cutting costs and increasing the efficiency and accuracy of its existing supply chain, it also wants to take advantage of the major appeal of smaller businesses. Smaller businesses are usually more specialized and offer unique value propositions: either new, exclusive, or exceptional products, or lower prices. These value propositions change frequently as trends rise and fall, and as competitive pressures alter price points. Infrastructure technology reaches Nirvana when companies like Wal-Mart can have the benefits of the real-time enterprise traditionally limited to a few key partners, while simultaneously having the flexibility to be opportunistic with small businesses. For example if Wal-Mart wanted to enter the market for high-fashion clothing it would seek to establish business process collaboration links with boutiques in Paris, Los Angeles, New York and London. In the fashion industry product lines are re-created afresh season-to-season—and with each re-design so too the design of their supply-chain. The fashion industry learned long ago that frequent and periodic supply-chain re-design allows them to reach out to niche designers and to specialist producers.

Paul Strassmann confirms, "Carr completely disregards the explosive growth of small businesses, a development made possible by the Internet. Information technology is a killer of bureaucracies and a reducer of overhead expenses; those qualities increase its microeconomic viability. Asserting that benefits will accrue only to the economy at large and not to individual firms is a prescription for opting out of the information-based competitive races in the years to come. Corporations are confronting increased uncertainty about markets, competition, resources, employee attitudes and the impact of legislation. The corporate environment requires more complex coordination that ever before, and there is less time for taking corrective measures. As a result there is a need for *more and better* information technologies."[49] Although Carr is wary of Strassmann's recommendation that "companies should be ready to engage in yet another IT investment cycle [of the right kind],"[50] Carr must be talking about Old IT, not the process management investments needed to cope with the realities of today's far-flung global competition.

The Universal Distribution Network Hasn't Caught Up With Demand

Third, when Carr states that "the capacity of the universal distribution network (the Internet) has caught up with demand—indeed, we already have considerably more fiber-optic capacity than we need," he excludes the realities of the global economy and this thing called the digital divide.

Even those 5.5 million firms in the U.S. that employ fewer than 100 people go sorely lacking and can only wish they had a fiber optic link into real-time value chains. For them it's often a shaky dial-up connection at best, even though they are the backbone of the economy. Fiber in the ground means little if the last mile for the small guy cannot be empowered or if there are insufficient IP addresses and network switches to enable a hundred to a thousand fold increase in individual uses and paths. Universal, high-bandwidth, last-mile connectivity, and deeper "business process enabled switching" are examples of Brian Arthur's 1001 sub-technologies. They and countless other innovations are what businesses need to ensure that IT is not a distraction and inconvenience to innovative employees trying to build effective supply networks to better serve their customers.

Perhaps it's not even more fiber that's needed for a buildout of infrastructural technologies. If you consider the possibilities of high-speed wireless access to the Internet, such as new G3 technologies, then even Carr's infrastructural technology buildout has only just begun. Ask small businesses in Calcutta or Cape Town if they have too much fiber-optic capacity. The State of the World Forum[51] reports that as of September 4, 2000:

- Human population of the world: 6,094,046,761
- World population with *access* to telephones: 20%
- World population connected to the Internet: 2%

It just may be that we are at the infantile stages of building infrastructural technologies.

The World Wants Commodity IT Suppliers

Fourth, when Carr says that "IT vendors are rushing to position themselves as commodity suppliers or even as utilities," business leaders that want to *use* their offerings for competitive advantage say, "it's about time." This is another issue with which the IT industry must deal, not the businesses that consume that industry's offerings for competitive advantage. The latter wants cheaper, better, faster IT, and have been waiting since the 1960s for the computer utility to actually happen. They say, "Bring it on, so we can use it to offer our distinctive business processes using the best IT at commodity prices." For the IT industry itself, commoditization is just part of the sweep of history and is precisely what is leading the industry to invent the new process technologies.

The Dot-Com Bubble Has Burst—So What?

Finally, Carr says, "and most definitely, the investment bubble has burst, which historically has been a clear signal that an infrastructional technology is reaching the end of its buildout." His leap from premise to conclusion is misleading. While the argument Carr puts forward and the debate generated from it is clearly riding the current backlash wave of the great IT overspend, industry veteran and author David R.R. Webber points out, "Wall Street caused the dot.bomb cycle because they have stupid people making technology decisions with other peoples' money. Still want to go with those guys' think tanks?"[52]

Arthur C. Clarke, distinguished author of science and fiction, including *2001: A Space Odyssey,* wrote, "Any sufficiently advanced technology is indistinguishable from magic."[53] The advent of the Internet followed by the ability to do instant e-commerce certainly worked magic on Wall Street where blind greed got the best of all those 401k funds that created too much money in public markets.

The irrational exuberance and technical naivety of the past in no way proves that infrastructional technology is reaching the end of its buildout—that's a spurious correlation. If anything it's only proof that there is a sad side of the human condition where magic and greed can blind the masses into failing to ask common-sense questions such as, "Where are the fundamental business models and business processes under all this dot-com hype?" Naturally, the markets corrected when unsound business models that twenty-something-year-old entrepreneurs had concocted were revealed.

Contrary to Carr's belief that the bursting of the investment bubble is "a clear signal that an infrastructional technology is reaching the end of its buildout," the exact opposite is almost certainly the case, and the IT buildout has only just begun.

Economist Brian Arthur believes that the information

technology revolution is now poised for a very long build-out period, much like the railroad industry in the 1850s. Later in a buildout, the technologies that first heralded the boom take hold, become widespread and realize their full potential. Their larger scale deployment is not based on irrational spending, but depends on deliberate engineering to ensure that the new technology meets the needs of society and is not a distraction to the activities it is there to support. In his article *Is the Information Revolution Dead?*[54] Arthur notes that, "all threads of thought on technology revolutions lead back to Austrian economist Joseph Schumpeter." A critic of Marx and Keynes, Schumpeter developed a sophisticated perspective for thinking about business cycles, political institutions and social processes in the modern world. Among his most important economic studies is *The Theory of Economic Development and Business Cycles.*

Schumpeter's theories of the *clustering of innovations* have also been studied by economists such as Carlota Perez and Chris Freeman of the Sussex school in England. Perez and Freeman have applied them to explain how each technological revolution gives rise to a paradigm shift and a "New Economy" and how these "opportunity explosions" (focused on specific industries) also lead to the recurrence of financial bubbles and crises. In their book, *Technological Revolutions and Financial Capital,* they take a long-term perspective on the good and bad times in the economy and link technology and finance to "patterns of speculative exuberance, followed by crash, followed by a strong build-out period." These findings are illustrated with examples from the past two centuries: the industrial revolution, the age of steam and railways, the age of steel and electricity, the emergence of mass production and automobiles, and the current information revolution knowledge society. These ideas appear to be the root of many of the railroad analogies in technology.

Arthur observes, "If we lay the information revolution alongside the great railway revolution in Britain, year for year, we'd now be somewhere around 1850—just after the railway investment mania of 1845 and its crash in 1847. ... What is interesting about both the canal and railway revolutions is that their crashes were by no means the end. In the decades after 1793, Britain went on to build out 2,000 miles of waterway, doubling its pre-crash mileage. And canals became the key infrastructure component of the Industrial Revolution. Similarly, in 1845, just before the crash, Britain possessed 2,148 miles of railway; 65 years later it had 21,000 miles. The major buildout of railways came *after* the crash of 1847. ... In the United States, there was no equivalent of the British railway mania. Certainly there were periods of setback in which railroad over investment was partly to blame. In the depression of 1859, the economic commentator Henry Carey Baird complained that 'our railroad system has cost more than $1,000,000 and has brought ruin upon nearly everyone connected with it, the nation included.' But, again, at this time railroads in the United States were just beginning. In 1860 the United States had 30,000 miles of built-out track; by 1914 it had 253,000 miles. The buildout, when it came, was massive."

Arthur's themes are echoed by Computer Sciences Corporation in its 2003 *Leading Edge Forum* report, "The time is ripe for networked business structures to emerge. ... Part of this buildout, then, is the networked business and the underlying IT architecture and technologies that support it. Think of business as being fundamentally based on the network and integrated with it, e.g., Amazon's Web Services program, rather than merely enabled by it, e.g., a link to Amazon's site, or connected to it, e.g., remote database access. As business rethinks itself in terms of the network, so must architecture. Truly networked business requires a much deeper commitment to multi-enterprise architecture that embraces many enterprises outside the box and emphasizes flexibility and reuse, in contrast to conventional inside the box single-enterprise architecture, which might have a controlled interface to a single system outside the box. The result is nothing short of an IT architecture rEvolution. The architecture rEvolution builds on existing technologies such as Internet protocols (evolutionary) to provide vastly new ways of operating (revolutionary). It is marked by increasingly distributed information systems, and with them, service-oriented and process-centric architectures."[55]

Wingham Rowan, producer and host of the 1990s British television program *cyber.café,* vividly describes a possible long-term consequence of the amenity-based IT buildout. In his book *Net Benefit: Guaranteed Electronic Markets,*[56] Rowan depicts an IT-enabled society that is far different from the simplistic visions of 1990s Web-based "net markets." Rowan envisions pervasive electronic markets underpinned and guaranteed by governments that are routinely used to trade everything from office space to bicycle rentals between individuals. Rowan paints a clear picture of the impact of such an IT infrastructure as having fundamental and social consequences.

Could similar marketplaces now be set up in which citizens could trade their periods of work, accommodation, transport, cash to lend and make countless other transactions with the protection and market access taken for granted by dealers in world currency markets. Rowan asks a difficult question "Could potent new trading technology be used to build national marketplaces that would then rewrite the rules of capitalism? In this scenario, banks, service industries and many government departments could become marginalized as individuals began effortlessly trading among themselves, the role of government, and companies in key sectors, to underwrite this economic activity of its citizens and employees."[57]

If Rowan's analysis is only half correct, the logical conclusion may be that government itself may be forced to recognize that IT, far from not mattering, is in fact the bedrock upon which tomorrow's capitalistic democracy critically depends. In this case, government would have to provide for IT-enabled marketplaces the same *critical infrastructure status* and protection it gives to other utilities such as electricity and water in the light of global terrorism.[58] Or could it be that, as Rowan says, "After a number of countries had a public guaranteed electronic markets system (GEMS) up and running with competing consortia demonstrating viable business models, remaining governments could be in the awkward position of justifying a decision to stay out of GEMS and deprive their populations of the benefits."[59]

Far from the impact of the IT buildout being "closer to it's end than its beginning," we tend to believe Don Tapscott when he states "We're at the beginning, not the end. We're in the first innings,"[60] and we believe Brian Arthur when he says "when that new phase comes forth, it will be a giant."[61] Rowan's visions may indeed be a glimpse of the true significance of information technology in the 21st century.

To summarize:

1. Scarcity may be the basis for sustainable competitive advantage in the physical world during the industrial revolution, but not so in the realm of human creativity and innovation in the information revolution.
2. Carr's article is really about the IT industry, not the use of IT for strategic advantage.
3. Infrastructural technologies provide their *users* opportunities for competitive advantage when they approach critical mass, not early in their development. First-stage advantages apply to the infrastructural providers, the IT industry.
4. Carr's article describes the last fifty years of the IT industry, more accurately called EDP.
5. Carr's argument does not recognize the significance of the business process, and instead focuses on "functional" IT applications and individual services.
6. Today's IT Utility is only the platform for tomorrow's BPM capability. Scale, standards, and access are valuable to store, process and transport unique business processes of distinction.
7. Web services are an emerging technology related to application integration, not to selling commoditized applications by some third-party IT utility company.
8. Best practices aren't the only practices, as Carr implies in his article. Companies need both best practice and

differentiating best-in-class business processes.

9. Many economic and technological signs indicate that the IT buildout is closer to its beginning that it is to its end. BPM both assists in facilitating the buildout, by standardizing process technologies, yet simultaneously enhances the ability of companies to differentiate when using infrastructural technologies.

A Closer Look at The Last Fifty Years of IT

Carr says information technology is a fuzzy term, and "it is used in its common current sense, as denoting the technologies for processing, storing and transporting information in digital form." The problem with this definition is that it does not define *information*. As revealed several times by comments, such as, "By now, the core functions of IT—*data* storage, *data* processing, and *data* transport—have become available and affordable to all," Carr reveals that he means *data* and the old world of *data processing*. Gartner gets it right, "Where Carr goes wrong is by equating IT with hardware and networks; rather, the essence of IT is *information*. Successful firms will use information and IT intelligently and in new ways to solve business problems and create customer value."[62]

For the past fifty years computers have indeed been seen as data machines, systems of record that reflect the results of after-the-fact business activity. Such data-centric thinking also includes passing of data, primarily in the form of standard documents between trading partners, a trend established years before the Internet with Electronic Data Interchange or EDI.

Carr is not alone in this flawed perception. Companies too are stuck in this data-centric vision of the IT role, in which there is an ever growing disconnect between the business and the technology it deploys. Because the data-centric paradigm of IT won't take us past where we are stuck today, *we must break it*, otherwise the buildout will stall and Carr's world will prevail.

Back in the 1950s there was the myth of the great thinking machine. Later the myth of MIS, the management information system, rose up to replace it. The reality, however, is that to this day, the majority of business computers are record-keeping machines, not management machines. They can take in, chew up and spit out trillions of bytes of *data*, but where is the management insight, the *actionable information* needed in context, and in real time at all levels of automated and human decision-making?

The strategic value of IT that moves it beyond commodity, and therefore beyond the risk averse, cost cutting, CIO, lies in information and beyond that, knowledge and *process*. Few companies have yet to achieve this. The methods, techniques and mindset of IT today remain fixated on static data—on its capture, storage and retrieval.

Two influences underlie this arrested development for the majority of companies. First computers were accounting machines, and the management theory that drove them was cost accounting: The lowest cost was equated with competitive advantage in the world of mass production. The second factor reinforcing the data-centric world of IT is that computers don't sense, reason and change course on the fly the way humans do. When early business technologists dreamed of machines that could do these things, they realized that their data-processing systems must separate data from processes, because only data could be structured in a stable, reliable and predictable way, a desirable quality in an accurate cost accounting system. We must now apply a similar technique to the representation of business processes. Based on discussions with leading CIOs, we believe that their ambitions for applying IT to business strategy lie far from Carr's data processing. The concerns of IT departments over which they preside are far from his definition of IT of the last fifty years.

Take just one *mandatory* concern: accountability. As companies intertwine their core operational and financial business processes to form virtual corporations that span entire value chains, new levels of transparency, management control and accountability are not just essential, they are being mandated. As Gartner says, "Every U.S. business must comply with thousands of federal business regulations. Process management technologies and business rules engines can help companies understand new rules and enforce compliance policy."

A similar phenomenon occurred when shared databases became widespread in the early 1980s and, spurred on by the Foreign Corrupt Practices Act and a spree of computer crime, led auditors to develop new methods and techniques to audit *through*, instead of *around*, database management systems. EDP Audit and Control became a certified practice among auditors, and EDP Auditors became a fixture in the courtroom. Today, new legal structures such as the Sarbanes-Oxley Act and the Basel Accord place greater emphasis upon internal controls, external audits and supervisory review processes. In short, business process management systems will shift regulatory, auditing and legal concerns from data to business processes, and the impact will be global. Addressing these business process concerns opens the door to the digitization of shared, multi-company business processes.

E-commerce, introduced to the world by Amazon.com, was the wake-up call that, for the first time, companies could do more than process and share data, they could also breathe life into their business processes, the end-to-end coordination of activities that deliver value to customers. On the other hand, the fundamental premises that Carr sets out relate to the data-centric paradigm of IT of the past fifty years. During this time, IT meant automating back office record keeping. Passing data between trading partners was the extent of collaborative commerce. This may have been reduced to best practice and become a required, but non-strategic, commodity, but Carr mistakenly extrapolates what this means for the future.

The future of IT is about the management of the business processes that companies use to coordinate internal work across functional stovepipes and to collaborate, compute and transact with customers and trading partners with transparency and accountability. Such end-to-end processes unify computing and communications, thereby bringing together what has previously been delivered using disparate and disjoint technology platforms to provide holistic information systems that are simultaneously:

- Automational, eliminating human labor from a process where it adds no value;
- Informational, capturing process information for purposes of understanding;
- Sequential, changing process sequence, or enabling parallelism;
- Tracking, closely monitoring process status and participants;
- Analytical, improving analysis of information and decision-making across processes;
- Geographical, coordinating processes across distances;
- Integrative, consolidating and integrating sub-processes and tasks;
- Intellectual, the process of capturing and distributing intellectual assets;
- Disintermediating, eliminating intermediaries from a process;
- Computational, performing calculations as part of a distributed process;
- Collaborative, allowing participants to manage sets of shared work processes; and
- Compositional, building new processes from elementary reusable process patterns

Beyond Data, On To Process Digitization

We are now at the cusp of a new opportunity for achieving strategic advantage through information technology. The key is to link organizational change, project management, automation and reengineering to create something genuinely new. By placing what Michael Hammer defines as "end-to-end work" at its center, the IT industry is now able to supply businesses with tools to support process work, not just work with data.

Today, businesses spend 30% of their IT budgets integrating their functional applications using enterprise application integration or EAI technology. Why are they going to all this effort and expense? They are tying together fragments of

functional applications to create end-to-end business processes—those activities that bring ultimate value to customers.
Indeed, it is the business process, not technology or a functional
application, that meets Michael Porter's criteria for sustainable
competitive advantage: distinction and fit. Porter argues that
business activities (business processes) are the basic building
blocks of competitive advantage. The ability to explicitly define
these work activities and manage them through successive improvement cycles, from conception to retirement, using digital
means, eluded IT during its first fifty years—but no longer.

Creating, deploying and optimizing end-to-end business
processes that are built, not just to last, but to adapt, is precisely
the state of IT thinking and direction today. But it's an undertak-
ing that has only just begun, for the digitization and management
of business processes has been far too complex in the past,
dominated as IT was by data-centric systems, databases and the
application paradigm built on top of data management.

In short, the vision of process management is not new, but
existing theories and IT systems have not been able to cope with
the reality of business processes—until now. By implementing
process management, corporations can gain the capabilities they
need to innovate, reenergize performance and deliver the value
today's markets demand. The breakthrough in business process
management (BPM) is its technology engine, the business
process management system (BPMS). With this new category of
enterprise information system and new process representations
based on a solid mathematical foundation, a completely new
form of *business process automation* can enable a completely new
source of competitive advantage.

BPM and its new technology engine do not represent another IT vendor's cheap trick or marketing ploy. It's vital to acknowledge the underlying science that makes them possible. Scientist Robin Milner had this to say about the repurposing of his
and others' work of the past twenty years, "I'm delighted that
Business Process Management and its modeling language have
found good use for the concepts of process calculus. For over

two decades the process calculus community has sought to combine two things: the way you define and analyze mobile distributed processes and the way you program them. We believe we've found the basic maths to meet this challenge, and it is heartening to hear that it is being applied to the management and automation of a company's most basic economic assets, its core processes. For computer scientists, the practical observation of the use of process calculus within the IT industry's newest software category, the business process management systems, will help us to deepen our theories, particularly in terms of higher level process representation. We aim not just to build, but also to understand, the colossal global computer in which we live. It is exciting that business systems can now not only use what we have done so far, but will also help us to come closer to our goal."

During the celebrations heralding the arrival of the twenty-first century, many companies were concerned that their industries might get "Amazoned," that a dot-com or net market just might turn their industry upside-down. But with the dot-com clutter cleared away, companies in all industries better be worried about getting "General Electrified." Jack Welch responded to the dot-com era with a destroy-your-company-dot-com initiative. GE's new CEO, Jeff Immelt, has taken the baton and expanded the company's original vision with the Digitization Initiative, which aims to digitize as many business processes as possible, especially those outward-facing processes used to actually conduct business with customers and trading partners. Analyst firm, Gartner, reinforces the prescription, "Direct new IT investments toward pre-sale, selling and other business processes largely untouched by IT so far."[63]

The differences between traditional data-centric software applications, and the coming process-centric systems are huge. Today, the vast majority of employees in large enterprises rely on nothing more than email, spreadsheets and word processing to *coordinate* their work. Beyond this, automation is provided by expensive software applications maintained solely in the data center and by the staff in the IT department. Yet the majority of the needed day-to-day automation tasks are modest in relation to the complexity of today's IT systems. For example, nearly everyone needs more visibility of and control over their interactions with colleagues, partners and customers. Such interactions and communications are indeed the essence of business processes. Business users need control of information flows so that everyone remains focused on the task and are coordinated with everyone else—business processes are organic, seldom follow a predefined pattern and cannot easily be packaged.

Carr states that "A few companies may still be able to wrest advantages from highly specialized applications that don't offer strong economic incentives for replication, but those firms will be the exceptions not the rule." He appears to assume that process automation will always be procured in the form of packaged software. But perhaps 80% of process-related tasks and their coordination can be designed and implemented by business people themselves—if only they had proper tools to give them direct manipulation of their business processes. Moreover, business people should be able to implement changes to live business processes.

BPM systems are already helping organizations obliterate, not just bridge, the business-IT divide by placing control of business processes directly in the hands of business people, including front-line workers. Personal, workgroup and departmental BPM tools, akin to tools commonly found in office productivity suites, are emerging. The role of IT is changing, away from custom development of more and more application software and toward the provision of BPM systems. Imagine a "Process Office" suite, providing an integrated, process-centric approach to collaboration, computation, work management, process modeling and simulation.

Imagine also a business system intended to support sales campaigns, but before you do, consider the sales campaign *processes*. Those processes are different in each industry; different for different classes of products and services; and different for different classes of customers. Selling a military aircraft is different than selling paint, which, in turn, is quite different from selling fashion goods or financial services. In addition, all companies have multiple customer segments. In the aerospace industry working with the government is different than working in the commercial sector. In the chemicals industry, working with wholesalers is different than working with farmers. Companies must even treat individual customers differently, at different points in the sale cycle, particularly as they close in on the sale.

Now think about building a computer system to support the sales campaign process. Given the differences across sectors, products, services and customers, can such sales processes be enshrined in packaged software? If so, how complex would the data model and software code have to be to support the flexibility the CIO will need to adapt the software to its circumstances and to the firm's own processes. No wonder CIOs often give up, preferring instead to find an off-the-shelf application close to their needs and then adapt to it, rather than even attempting to adapt the packaged software to the unique practices of the business. Painful organizational changes are necessary in order to restructure work around the packaged applications, further complicating deployment.

Fortunately, these are compromises companies need make no longer, given BPM. And the significance goes right to the heart of the debate on the strategic value of IT, for BPM resets the business-IT equation by placing control of process elements directly in the hands of the business, taking them away from constraints set by IT vendors.

Companies in different industries have diverse needs for sales campaign automation. Individual companies in the same sector compete with each other by differentiating the sales process. As each campaign progresses, processes associated with prospective customers may need to vary significantly from initial sales plans. The plan, which is the process, almost always has to change. For these reasons, packaging the sales campaign processes in static software code with a static data model is inappropriate.

Instead of packaging the sales campaign as a software application, why not deliver it as a business process? Give business people the tools they need to build processes. Allow them to customize a process for each customer. Give them the tools to include participants in the campaign as required, including employees, partners, systems and information sources. Let the BPM system manage the end-to-end state of all processes. Provide business managers the tools they need to query the state of the campaign along key dimensions such as customer, product, part and, based on this business intelligence, to make adjustments to the process in order to respond to individual customer needs.

The differences between the sales processes in different sectors, for different products and for different customers, as well as the adjustments to the process necessary at different stages in the sales lifecycle, apply across a whole range of business processes much wider than the IT industry has thus far been willing to admit. What the IT industry refers to by three letter acronyms such as ERP, CRM, SCM and PLM, are in fact relatively hard-coded software systems that provide only the lowest common denominator functions that apply to all companies—at a stretch.

On the other hand, GE's automated business processes are now required to provide their own analytics and change levers so that its business leaders can have the personalized digital cockpit instruments they need to navigate their organizations through turbulent times, in real time. As far as providing feedback of results with digital dashboards, BPM should also stand for business *performance* management, for the process lifecycle enables what the IT press colloquially calls business activity monitoring (BAM). Business activity monitoring is dependent upon the end-to-end visibility of the past, present and future state of process execution; and the process design audit trail—all features of a proper BPM system.

GE is intent on making course corrections daily or weekly, rather than monthly or quarterly, thereby saving time and money and better serving its customers. GE gets IT. The firm understands the new process-based battlefront of business. GE saved $1.6 billion from process digitization, roughly 16% of the $10 billion it expects to save annually by 2006. $100 million was freed up by digitizing inventory, accounts payable and receivables (operational hyper-efficiency), and a salesperson can handle up to twice as many customers (hyper-effectiveness). But these are just the first tiny steps for BPM.

On today's battleground for economic growth, sustainability and innovation, companies like GE are arming themselves with explicitly defined business processes that can be manipulated on a scale previously unimaginable. Taking this perspective, Carr's *data-centric* analysis of IT looks increasingly off the mark. To understand why, we need to examine additional aspects of the relationship of the IT industry to business.

A Deeper Look at Commoditization Trends in IT

1. There is no single commodity

"Like many broadly adopted technologies ... IT has become a commodity." With this statement Carr applies one *commoditization timeline* to all of "IT," ignoring its constituent parts. What Carr dismisses as IT commodity is a complex mix of computing, communications and coordination—multi-faceted and multi-layered—consisting of elementary components of both hardware and software, woven together, providing the rich tools that businesses now enjoy. While some IT elements are commodities, others are not. Web Services pioneer Rajiv Gupta says, "Yes, Nicholas [Carr] is right, there is commoditization within the IT stack. Raw storage bits, raw processing power are good examples. However it is a little short sighted to then use that brush to paint all of IT. There are large swaths of the IT stack—especially in how one manages these components, how one connects them, the business processes that then run on the connected components—that are very strategic today. Will these get commoditized sometime in the future? Some of them perhaps. But not today."[64]

"IT Shouldn't Matter!" says Matthew Pryor, senior product architect at Versata and a BPMI.org board member. "While Carr's argument points to the complexity of IT and the frustration companies feel then it is a point well-made. However, the response should not be to cease investment in IT, but rather to eradicate complexity through the intelligent deployment of new approaches such as Business Process Management."[65] Gupta agrees, "I think a more insightful comment from Carr would have been that until now we have not managed to get the full strategic value from IT because the cost and complexity of getting things to work together have been such an impediment." Put another way, Forrester's Colony says "When it comes to IT spending, it's not 'more is better,' it's 'better is better.'"

Today, at companies such as JP Morgan, DuPont and BAE Systems there is little talk of Carr's "data processing." There is much talk of information, some of knowledge and growing talk of process. Yet Carr's article can confuse its readers by lumping data, technology, hardware, software, information, knowledge and process under the all-embracing IT moniker, which is a convenient label for those to whom it has become fashionable to question investment in *any* IT. Paul Strassmann puts it succinctly, "Information technologies now provide the primary means for extending the value of a firm's knowledge capital. They help companies manage the exploding accumulation of scientific, research, customer, engineering, property and intellectual assets. Corporations are confronting increased uncertainty about markets, competition, resources, employee attitudes and the impact of legislation. The corporate environment requires more complex coordination than ever before, and there is less time for taking corrective measures. As a result, there is a need for more and better information technologies."[66]

Would JP Morgan regard its software investments as a commodity, the investment that enables it to offer financial services worldwide? Would DuPont regard its data mining capabilities as a commodity, the decades of experience that enable the deep search for new industrial compounds? Would BAE Systems regard the algorithms and manufacturing-integrated design tools as a commodity, the capabilities it uses to design aircraft? Pryor continues, "Carr talks about IT no longer being scarce and therefore having less strategic significance, but what is his basis for comparison between each of the IT elements labeled as IT commodity? On what basis and by which definition does Carr create IT commodity categories?"

Today, it is true that companies regard items such as the Microsoft desktop, the Linux operating system, Internet protocols and Intel hardware as akin to commodities, but the argument stops there. When Carr generalizes that "IT has become a commodity" is he referring to everything that exists in the IT industry? If so, he must be implying the absence of innovation in that industry, which, frankly, doesn't wash.

2. Today's commodity was yesterday's innovation

There is only one mention of "innovation" in Carr's article. It is used primarily to refer to "economies of scale and brand recognition" achieved by early IT adopters and of which he says "proved more enduring than the original technological edge." But today's (simpler, lower cost) commodity was yesterday's (complex, more expensive) strategic *platform,* and this process continues today and forever. For example, twenty years ago, relational database management systems (RDBMS) were the innovation that emerged atop the low cost, standards-based, commodity operating system, Unix. In turn, the RDBMS-Unix combination replaced the more complex, more expensive, hierarchical database systems that could only operate in proprietary computer environments.

Judging by the wealth of Oracle's Larry Ellison, as well as the myriads of business applications that have been built atop databases (including the narrowly defined and packaged categories of ERP, SCM, CRM, PLM) the RDBMS could be argued to be one of the most successful categories of business software ever! But today the majority of business view relational databases as an affordable commodity.

Dan Faber, writing at ZDnet states, "We know a lot about automating processes with computers, but we are just at the beginning of *automating computing itself,* which is an essential step in its evolution. In that scenario, several layers of IT can be viewed as a commodity—as a common foundation upon which new, strategically important technology innovations will arise."[67] Faber has stepped right into the BPM arena and what has come to be called model-driven and design-driven architectures and programming techniques.

There are strong reasons to believe that the BPMS is going to be just as successful as the RDBMS, for the BPMS is perfectly suited to exploit the current commodity environment, including public and private networks, and Web services. Computer Sciences Corporation calls such pervasive environments the "Architecture rEvolution,"[68] which forms the substrate of each company's IT-enabled value chain and upon which they build and operate their own differentiated business processes. Unlike e-business technologies of the past, such as EDI and RosettaNet, there is no longer a need to agree on standard, undifferentiated, processes in order to interact with suppliers, partners and customers. Instead, connectivity standards provide the value-chain "dial tone" for companies. BPM systems are based, not on standard processes, but on a standard way to represent (and therefore to create, integrate, customize, transform etc.) all processes.

Like other IT innovations that created a *platform shift,* the purpose of BPM is not the replacement of pre-existing information systems, but rather their amplification, integration, customization and manipulation. Again, Gupta says, "Carr seems to be missing the forest for the trees. It is not, and never was, the fact that you chose Hitachi memory over Toshiba memory that gave you strategic advantage. So it is not as if there was strategic advantage at one point and now, because of commoditization, we are losing it. It always was how you used that memory, what data you chose to store in it, what information (or knowledge) you gleaned from that data, how you applied that information, how quickly and with what relevance the information was used at the time and place of most value, that was, and still is, of strategic value."

Forrester's CEO George F. Colony, talks about the IT iceberg, "Think of corporate IT as an iceberg, with the standardized technology below the water line and the non-standardized stuff above. The best CIOs are always jumping up and down on top of the IT iceberg to get it lower in the water, to get more technology fully standardized within their company. CIOs like Peter Solvik at Cisco and Dennis Jones at FedEx (both of whom have since moved on) were big iceberg dunkers... Low icebergs have two effects: decreased costs and higher flexibility ... High performing CIOs don't wake up worrying about which server to buy; they are fixated on how to use the 'above the water line' tech to nail the competition. The biggest payoff of low icebergs is that IT resources are freed up to focus above the water line where it is snowing, where new technology is emerging."[69] The BPM system reuses and repurposes the myriad existing stove-piped, data-centric, "functional" IT applications—what Carr refers to as "more liability than asset." Today, this strategy also applies to business process outsourcing where a *process neutral* interoperable infrastructure can allow the business to innovate with above-the-water-line processes, using business process management.

3. Core versus context, mission-critical versus support

In setting out his arguments for the role of IT in business, Carr does not take into account the difference between Geoffrey Moore's notions of *core* (those activities that differentiate you from competitors) and *context* (those activities that don't). Carr's notion of "IT as commodity" lies uneasily with such modern business theories, for to claim as such implies that *all* of IT is now contextual. What about the network management capabilities that allow telecommunications operators to provide service? What about the IT inherent to modern manufacturing systems as operated by contract manufacturers? Carr's argument describes the broad-brush sweep of history and does not take these differences into account.

There are few, if any, shades of gray in Carr's notion of commodity. Moore identifies the separate notions of *mission-critical* (those activities that pose a direct risk to your whole business if compromised) and *support* (those that do not)[70] as orthogonal to core and context. Carr never mentions such differences in his "IT Doesn't Matter" article, nor the *role* of IT in core *and* contextual business activities. For some companies IT itself is core, for others, it's contextual.

The advice we get from Carr is that IT must be protected via risk management. But every CIO knows there are some aspects of IT that are mission critical and some that are support. Today, it is normal practice to apply different business and IT protection, procurement and operations strategies to different elements of the IT and applications portfolio. Smart CIOs go to the dominant, market-leading vendors for Colony's below-the-water-line IT and buy based on price and service for "below the water line, IT doesn't matter … but there's a blizzard above the water line."[71]

4. Value from outsourcing

Carr's argument does not take into account the dynamics and benefits of IT outsourcing, and the symbiotic relationship between companies and their IT suppliers. Today companies enjoy a rich palette of outsourcing options and many are more interested in information solutions than technology for technology's sake. This trend will continue as the true infrastructural buildout gathers momentum and the IT industry continues to mature. Those IT companies that offer value-based solutions will be those that endure—commodity or luxury aside.

Companies that view IT skills as contextual in their business may choose to outsource IT in support of their core activities. They base their decisions on their concern over their ability to provide adequate IT services while focusing on the core business. Since their core business depends on automation, such companies will look for mission-critical IT providers, even across areas Carr may regard as just commodities.

Companies may view all of IT as contextual and a support function, in which case they enjoy multiple outsourcing options from a wide range of providers. Others may selectively outsource, identifying areas of the business where the decision to outsource IT is not as critical but the benefits are high in terms of the resources freed up.

Even companies that regard IT as core to their business, such as financial institutions (on the basis that money today is nothing more than digital bits) may nevertheless turn to IT outsourcing to provide capabilities beneath the tip of Colony's IT iceberg, at lower levels of the IT stack. A biscuit maker observed that its business is a commodity business, based on the use of commodity ingredients, yet it's core to them. Dell might say the same thing about the computers is sells. Does that mean the associated IT is a commodity? It depends upon who provides the service and whether their business model drives towards commodity.

It is no longer only IT that's being outsourced but business processes as well. Business Process Outsourcing (BPO), on a global scale, is well underway, and the implications are monumental. That last customer service call you made to Amazon.com, or British Airways, or General Electric could well have been handled in Bangalore, India, with the customer service representative (CSR) speaking in a Midwest, Johnie Carson, accent. Even more significant is that the CSR could fire off the appropriate business processes, in real time, to satisfy your unique and immediate needs right there in Columbus, Ohio.

Procurement expert Stan Lepeak paints a concise picture of how businesses are changing through outsourcing, "Organizations strive to excel at one or two core processes, e.g., customer care, or research and development, and to direct as many resources to those processes as possible. Furthermore, operating in today's global, high-tech and complexly regulated economy has become so complex that no organization can host internally all the skills and processes it needs to compete. Once a process is digitized, an organization can 'unplug' and outsource it to a third party for management."[72]

Far from not mattering, IT is critical to the business models of Global 2000 companies in two ways. First, since business services today are highly if not completely dependent upon automation, the "IT outsource" plays a key role in any decision to outsource a business process or business service. Second, the management of business process outsourcing is itself IT intensive. Where companies once outsourced well-defined, bounded, functional business domains (and the associated stovepipe IT applications) process management lets companies bundle, unbundle and rebundle the *end-to-end* processes they choose to outsource and with finer granularity. Outsourcing is becoming more collaborative, and value-chain integration is growing more dependent on business process management.[73]

To summarize:

- All of IT cannot be lumped into one commodity bucket.
- Carr's argument puts all aspects of the IT industry on the same commoditization trajectory.
- Carr's argument omits the cycles of innovation in the IT industry, building new innovations on commodity platforms, which were once key innovations themselves.
- The role of IT is not as simplistic as Carr's headline implies. It is necessary to distinguish between core, context, mission-critical and support IT activities.
- Carr does not describe outsourcing as a viable strategy by which companies can take advantage of commoditization trends in different parts of the industry.
- There is a crucial role for IT in the collaborative management of outsourced business processes, a huge growth area.

The *Invisible* "P" in IT Matters

Carr's article does not present new information. Professor Vijay Gurbaxani, Director of Research on IT and Organizations at the University of California, Irvine, points out that "many of the same points were made by Max Hopper in HBR in 1990, the same year Hammer published his seminal article 'Don't Automate, Obliterate.' In 'Rattling SABRE – New Ways to Compete on Information' he also argued that computing was becoming a utility. So these arguments aren't new."[74] Perhaps it is forever to be our fate and delight that HBR will, once every ten years or so, publish articles that create controversy, not so much by the content or logic of their argument, but by the nature of their subjects, headlines and because of the beguiling quality of their presentation.

Alan Greenspan has argued recently that, contrary to Carr's beliefs, "there are still significant opportunities for firms to upgrade the quality of their technology and with it the level of productivity."[75] Bill Gates appears to agree, stating that the software industry is on the verge of delivering an entirely new type of software that will change the dynamics of electronic commerce and many business processes. He says, "this is where I think in some ways people are really underestimating what can be done."[76]

We are on the cusp of a major shift in IT where the invisible "P" in "IT" really matters. Here is the equation:

Past 50 years	Next 50 years
T is the commodity	D+T is the commodity
"I" really means "D" (data = information out of context)	"I" means "P" (process = information in context)
"IT" is in reality "DT"	"IT" is in reality "PT" (or BPM)

If you are not into reading tables, *InformationWeek's* Bob Evans offers a tongue-in-cheek explanation of the concepts in a hypothetical meeting on the topic of business technology (BT), "Well, if Data Processing and DP gave way to IS and that gave way to IT and that's being overtaken by BT because the job is about the business, then shouldn't we also think that the emphasis should be about the B (the business) that can be enabled by the T (the technology)? And if that's true, then the technology is a means to an end, and that end is business success and profitability and growth, and the way to get there is by doing what we do as well as we can, and that means constantly innovating and improving how we work, and that means BPO, (business process optimization)."

"Poetry—pure poetry!" replied a co-worker.

"Aw, pipe down and stick with me. Here's the point: We made the shift from focusing on IT to focusing on BT, but in doing so, we've also gotta take fully into account the human behaviors that this BT stuff is supposed to improve and optimize—the business processes. They've gotta be improved constantly, relentlessly, and both inside our company and outside, as well among our customers and their customers and our suppliers and other partners. BT and BTO are enormously important, but they've gotta serve the greater cause of BPO, which in turn bows down to the great god of business. Because without that tightly coupled linkage, we're gonna go the way of all one-hit wonders."[77]

Indiana University's Associate Vice President, Bradley Wheeler, adds to this perspective, "IT is not Information Systems (IS) any more than advertising is marketing or bank accounts are finance. IT—"the boxes and wires"—is indeed the simple commodity building blocks for value-creating information systems. The strategic potential lies in timely and skillful use of these systems."[78]

BPM rests upon everything Carr thinks is now a commodity: open standards, global networks and common services. The value in IT has never been the wire, but what happens over the wire. Today, companies no longer seek to transport and manipulate data alone, they want to transport and manipulate persistent business processes, sharing them in a controlled fashion with customers, trading partners and suppliers. Business processes put information in the context of its use.

As we're confident Carr would remind us, email is now a commodity, as evidenced by the choice companies such as British American Tobacco make to outsource their email service to email service providers such as Interliant. But the conversations that take place over the outsourced email service are hardly about a commodity—they are about the lifeblood at BAT. Although Carr makes a strong case that certain aspects of IT have become commodities, what he misses is the significance of commodities when they meet and combine with new innovations. For email, the critical innovation was the Internet itself, creating both unique email addresses for all and therefore opening global collaboration and interaction across corporate firewalls.

It is the combination of digital capabilities that creates new value. It was not the development of the personal computer that led to the personal computing revolution. It was the world's first spreadsheet, VisiCalc. In the early 1970s, personal computers were the toys of hobbyists and nerds who loved to tinker with programs written in BASIC. Corporations went to great lengths to keep these toys out of their offices because, if they were to be put to any business use, the business would have to budget for a vast effort from IT to program them for each and every user. Enter VisiCalc.

VisiCalc gave business people the ability to manipulate the familiar rows and columns of data directly, a model that business people immediately understood, and the ability to use familiar formulas to build what-if analyses aimed at optimizing results. No programming needed—simply design and, presto, calculate! VisiCalc introduced a level of simplicity and convenience that was simply irresistible. It took 20 hours of work per week and turned it out in 15 minutes or less ... and let everyone become much more creative. The convenience and low cost of the breakthrough was striking, but the spreadsheet could not have been successful had it not been for the fact that personal computers—a standards-based commodity—were spreading like wildfire. To the business, the PC loaded with a spreadsheet meant a radical simplification of routine calculations, transferring to the everyday businessperson a function that had once required special programming skills. It took the IT department off the critical path of personal computing and launched a revolution. A similar revolution occurred as a result of the relationship between Unix and the relational database, which gave value to operating systems and spawned ten thousand "applications."

Today, a similar symbiotic relationship has emerged between Web Services and BPM. For, as the management prophets foretell, the next phase of corporate development will require systematic control of the value chain, rather than narrow-gauge process fixes. Michael Hammer has admitted that managing such wholesale change is mind-numbingly complex. In fact, it is no longer possible without computer assistance. What the spreadsheet did for numerical computation and the database management system for data manipulation, BPM will do for all process work. Since the management of business processes is the bulk of all work, subsuming computing and communication, BPM has a bright future.

Now "P", "I" *and* "T" combine to form the inseparable triad of business change. Alter the balance, and chaos and waste are sure to follow. For example, companies recently pumped indecent amounts of money into technology, trying to renew and reinvigorate their businesses by technological means alone. Forrester Research calculated the U.S. technology overspend for the years 1998 to 2000 at $65 billion, as large companies engaged in a historic tech orgy. Forrester's CEO, George Colony described the result, "Bewildered CEOs and CFOs who felt burned by the dollars lost (and who are now slowing capital spending to a trickle), lost credibility for IT, lost stature for vendors, hardware

for sale on eBay at 10 cents on the dollar, and pressure on operating margins. Oh, and by the way, you also get one toxic technology recession."[79] Indeed, it's the invisible "P" that determines
appropriate investments in IT.

Carr is right, "IT Doesn't Matter," so long as we interpret
the "I" in "IT" as data. But just as the "D" in IT gave way to
Information so will the "I" give way to the "P" and become a
commodity. The invisible "P" in IT can never be a commodity
for companies will always compete on the basis of unique and
distinctive business processes. "T" is just a platform and has no
value without the "P" in BPM.

Beyond Data Processing, On To BPM

If we take Carr's definition of data-centric IT at face value,
then the next fifty years will indeed be boring, as he asserts IT
must become. On the other hand, here are the new things
companies now need:

- A means not only to conceive of new processes, but to
  actually put them into action.
- A systematic method of analyzing the impact of business
  processes and a more reliable way of introducing new process
  designs.
- Executable process models that are aligned with business
  strategy, reflecting the complexity of everyday business
  activity and amenable to complete analysis, transformation
  and mobilization.
- A managed portfolio of excellent business processes, not only
  with the customer's current needs built-in, but also with
  "change built in."
- The ability to respond to the new invisible hands of the
  market—the abilities to combine and to customize processes.
- The transformation of organizational change from an impre-
  cise art with unpredictable outcomes into an engineering
  discipline with measurable outcomes.
- A counterpoint to the creativity and innovation of reengineer-

ing and the acceleration of all process improvement projects
and activities.

▪ An understanding of a company's trajectory in the process
economy—expanding markets and increasing profits, or de-
clining influence, roadblocks, over-capacity or failure to
respond to market shifts.

▪ A pervasive, resilient and predictable means for the processing of business processes, a permanent business change labo-
ratory, enabling ongoing innovation, transformation and
agility.

Business process processing should not be confused with
automation. Digital process models, while managed by IT, may
have little to do with Carr's conclusions about the value of IT.
The veteran business process improvement practitioner, Andrew
Spanyi, explains in his book, *Business Process Management is a Team
Sport[80]*, that "the ability to *execute* on strategy is the litmus test of
great strategy ideas, and that test comes from tightly linking enterprise business processes to strategy formulation. Great ideas
are one thing, the ability to execute on them means technology-
enabled business process management."

BPM doesn't automatically mean automation, for in a given
situation, all the relevant business processes just may be human-
driven processes. Herein lies one of the greatest misconceptions
about the forthcoming role of IT, for when the word *process* is
used, IT practitioners and IT analysts alike immediately assume
automation, that is, the execution of the process to replace human endeavor. Rather, IT will be used, in its business process
management form, to discover, model, manage and improve
processes that may have nothing whatsoever to do with "automation" but a lot to do with what Geary Rummler and Alan
Brache refer to as the "white space on the organization
chart"[81]—those elements of work that fall between systems and
departments and teams and that are based on communication,
coordination and cooperation.

Gartner's Yefim V. Natis explains, "Some of the most-elaborate business processes originated in ancient Mesopotamia and Egypt (there had to be a fairly sophisticated engineering, supply chain and human resources process behind the building of the Pyramids.) A business process is the essence of all business, then and now. Automation of business processes can push an industry into a new era (the way Henry Ford's assembly line revolutionized the automobile industry first and the whole society later.) A new phenomenon of business process automation is taking place in front of our eyes."[82] Indeed, BPM makes no assumption of whether any business process is automated or manual, or, typically, a combination of both. The business practice of BPM is undoubtedly amplified by the use of appropriate IT tools and the "M" in BPM has, over the years, morphed from "modeling to management." [83]

While automation can be readily achieved with a raft of existing technologies, many of them yielding brittle, hard-coded systems, BPM encompasses the executive, administrative and supervisory control over processes to ensure that they remain compliant with business objectives. *Business processes are the main intellectual property and competitive differentiator manifest in all business activity, and companies must treat them with a great degree of skill and care.*

Merely perfecting a business process in terms of meeting requirements at a given time is a necessary, but insufficient, response to the challenge of *change*. Processes cast in stone through point solutions, one-time projects, habitual work practice or the straightjacket of packaged business software can be, as Carr observed, as much a liability as an asset, no matter how excellent they may be. For if incumbent companies are to compete against market disrupters large or small, they must exploit inherent advantages of the implicit processes embedded within their experience, their assets and their relationships. For this to happen, processes must be explicit. In short, companies must obliterate the business-IT divide, transforming legacy systems into assets, via process digitization, rather than treating them as liabilities.

If this seems extreme, consider that the majority of all

modern management theories—reengineering, process innovation, total quality management, Six Sigma, activity-based costing, value-chain analysis, cycle-time reduction, supply-chain management, excellence, customer-driven strategy and management by objectives—have stressed the significance of the business process and its management. In light of this, it seems surprising that the IT industry has up to now delivered only "business applications," small fragments of end-to-end processes capable of nothing more than manipulating static business data using pre-packaged procedures.

All information systems are imperfect simulations of the businesses they support. Companies are coming to understand that the principles of inter-connected and inter-related processes are the reality behind today's IT-facade. This change from applications to business processes at the heart of digital systems is structural—a shift in the tectonic plates that underlie the business-technology equation. It will only come about by abandoning the assumption that business information systems design must be based on the separate notions of data, procedure and communication. Investment in information technology can no longer be justified if business systems remain a weak and incomplete representation of the CEO's strategy. There must be a paradigm shift in the quality and expression of business processes if companies are to apply systematic methods to their development and execution—in strategy, in practice and in information technology.

Two decades ago companies implemented data management systems, and a common relational data model, because they recognized the value of business data and the data problems they would face if data continued to be embedded in each separate business application. As companies face their process future, similar pressures are at work, creating the demand for the business process management.

The Process is the Product

The strategy firm McKinsey & Company publishes many

reports analyzing the strategic value of IT and its management. McKinsey maintains that competitive advantage consists of the progress a company makes as its competitors, paralyzed by confusion, complexity and uncertainty, sit on the sidelines.[84] According to their view, the key to success is to be ready to act as soon as it becomes possible to estimate, with reasonable accuracy, the risks and rewards of an investment in process. This depends upon the availability of information to make decisions and the ability to change business processes with agility.

CEOs who therefore approach corporate IT strategy as a portfolio of initiatives, each aimed at achieving favorable outcomes for the entire enterprise, can extend this approach to the high-level management of a portfolio of business processes. To achieve the desired outcomes, a company must manage its process portfolio with the same rigor that a venture capital firm uses to manage its portfolio of investments. They must organize a disciplined search for the best processes, inside and outside the firm; nurture and enhance promising processes; and consider the option of acquiring process from third parties through collaboration, purchase or alliance (outsource, insource.) In so doing, they must take account of Carr's commoditization effects. The question for CIOs is, "What role will the IT function play in the gathering process agenda?"

While Carr chooses to marginalize IT and CIOs by minimizing their role as one of the key inspirations and sources of strategic value in business, deep interaction between the CEO and the CIO has been common for some time. For example, General Motors' CIO has, for a long time, teamed each of his group CIOs with specific department heads, seeking further understanding of and alignment with the business they are serving, and seeking the ability to jointly innovate solutions. This makes sense, for products and services are only the by-product of processes. In every case, the process *is* the product. With the start of World War II, no longer did coal and iron go in one end of Ford's River Rouge plant and automobiles come out the other, tanks rolled off the assembly line. Ford's product was, indeed, its vehicle manufacturing process.

Lepeak again, "The G2000 organizational model continues to evolve from insular and self-sufficient to open and specialized. Gone are the highly vertically integrated business and organizational models of the early to mid 20th century. ... More recently, organizations have been getting out of the business of managing their facilities, logistics and back-office operations. Organizations today are focusing on a narrowing set of core competencies. Already many supply chain functions are being outsourced, including inventory management, transportation services, and even manufacturing. What's driving this trend is the fact that competitive differentiation is increasingly a function of horizontal business process expertise and not vertical integration."[85] For each decision taken to outsource, another company takes an in-source. Therefore, commoditization, rather than being isolated to the IT industry, occurs across the board but is inextricably linked to IT. Successful organizations do not, unlike Carr's analysis, separate IT decisions from other strategic thought. No longer do organizations throw information system requirements over the wall to IT.

Capital One, a large bank and credit card marketer is still increasing its information technology spending. The firm is famous for its use of data mining and information analysis techniques to find and reach particularly profitable slices of the credit card market. The company has an *information-based strategy* in which technology and business considerations are deeply intertwined. "Capital One is growing strongly and its technology spending will rise 10 to 20 percent this year,"[86] said Gregor Bailar, the company's chief information officer. While some aspects of IT best practices may be commodities today, and that is only natural, IT is mostly used strategically to blend business services to form business processes of distinction. By doing so, companies are embedding information processing capabilities in products and services. So, far from IT not mattering, it is intrinsic to business success.

In the 1950s, a young Ronald Reagan hosted the top-ranked television program, *General Electric Theater*, and made GE's slogan famous: "Progress is our most important product." If that program were on TV today, the new slogan would no doubt be, "Process is our most important product." Good processes don't make winning companies; winning companies make good processes, using business ingenuity *and* IT.

Beyond the IT Shop,
On To The Process Office

We conjecture that the "I" in IT has already been supplemented by the "P" in BPM. A new discipline is emerging in many companies and is embodied in the *Process Office.* British American Tobacco, Astra Zeneca, GE, Shell, IBM, Schneider, Merck and a host of other companies have already established business process management (BPM) centers of excellence to spearhead their Digitization efforts and to capture, and then disseminate, best-in-class processes across the firm from wherever they originate. Such companies are organizing around Hammer's notion of end-to-end work, as opposed to functional specialization, and subsequently striving for improvement using process management methods and tools. In doing so these companies blend business *and* IT within *innovation programs,* creating new processes and implementing additional measurement (Key Performance Indicators) and adjustment controls over existing processes. They are using process lifecycle models such as Six Sigma to help guide these activities. How different this is from IT being regulated to risk mitigation and cost control!

As Gartner reported in June 2003, "We are seeing BPM embedded in nearly every package solution and many horizontal technology offerings today. Many BPM pilot projects have evolved into more-impressive solutions, with positive case studies abounding. An example is the reduction of cost of claims processing by 20 percent in a property and casualty insurance company, with the claims processing requiring just one-third the time. Although the example is in the insurance industry, where BPM is strong, we are seeing uptake in use and benefits in the banking, finance, credit card, healthcare, pharmaceutical, government and discrete manufacturing industry sectors as well."

"Because BPM delivers solid ROI and both short-term and long-term VOI, we expect the business to gravitate to its use, and we expect process optimization to become a habit in many enterprises, driven by compliance acts and quality initiatives such as Six Sigma projects. In addition, we anticipate that many enterprises will use streamlined processes as a competitive weapon in the marketplace."[87]

Twenty years ago, during the IT era Carr discusses, IT was an add-on, dealing only with parts of end-to-end processes and used only in IT's traditional role of automation. Today IT is intrinsic, and its role extends to the total process lifecycle. It is hard to imagine a significant commercial product or service that is not inextricably linked to, and dependent upon, computing and communication: examples include cars, mobile phones, logistics, travel, health and financial services. Robin Milner's *Informatics,* the process-based unification of computing and communication, truly reflects the engine of commerce that it enables. By contrast, Carr's article obsesses about external commodity items such as data stores, data networks and data processing. It is clearly time to move on from the IT shop to the process office.

The New Value in "IT of a Different Kind"

Playing somewhat to the gallery, and echoing commonly held beliefs about corporate overspend in IT, Carr's jibes, "Every year, businesses purchase more than 100 million PCs, most of which replace older models. Yet the vast majority of workers who use PCs rely on only a few simple applications— word processing, e-mail, spreadsheets, and Web browsing. These applications have been technologically mature for years; they require only a fraction of the computing power provided by today's microprocessors. Nevertheless, companies continue to roll out across the board hardware and software upgrades." Ed Benincasa, vice president of MIS (IT) at FN Manufacturing Inc., was quoted as saying, "[that] when he looks around at the company's accumulated technology, much of it has lost the luster of competitive edge, including PCs, printers, servers and storage. ... PCs, they used to be maybe considered a competitive edge, you had it; somebody else didn't. Nowadays, it's almost a mandatory tool, like a telephone. You can't survive without them."[88]

It's easy to pick fights with the IT industry and get the likes of Bill Gates and Steve Ballmer to fire back, by appealing to CFOs burdened by IT costs. "Big hardware and software suppliers have become very good at parceling out new features and capabilities in ways that force companies into buying new computers, applications, and networking equipment much more frequently than they need to. ... The time has come for IT buyers to throw their weight around, to negotiate contracts that ensure the long-term usefulness of their PC investments and impose hard limits on upgrade costs," Carr says.

No one disagrees that the IT industry must continuously evaluate its value proposition. Carr is reporting on real concerns, as evidenced by Bill Joy's comments at 2003 World Economic Forum[89] in Davos. As chief scientist and cofounder of Sun Microsystems, a company with much to lose if IT continues to tip downward, Joy asked "What if the reality is that people have already bought most of the stuff they want to own?" Indeed, what does the IT industry do if this is true?

Vendors like Microsoft are evolving to survive in this commoditized environment by turning its Office suite into an annual subscription service, an observation interpreted by Carr as "tacit acknowledgement that companies are losing their need—and their appetite—for constant upgrades." True enough. But isn't this about Corporate IT Procurement Policy rather than a signal that information technology does not matter?

Some companies indeed paid insufficient attention to what they were buying during the boom years, (and much software lies dormant on shelves today) but companies could never buy competitive advantage by buying IT. To understand how the IT industry can make genuine steps forward, as opposed to papering over the cracks by peddling simpler PCs and software rental schemes that amortize upgrade costs, we need to look outside the IT industry altogether.

The advent of computer aided design and computer as-sisted manufacturing (CAD/CAM) brought major new efficien-cies to industrial engineering, starting with the aerospace and automotive industries, and later spreading to all industries based on product design. At the outset, reductions in concept to pro-duction time were of the order of 25 to 50 percent. As the new approach matured, ten-fold and even hundred-fold reductions were achieved. Collaboration was vastly simplified as suppliers and specialists in a given industry adopted new tools based on standards such as STEP (the Standard for the Exchange of Product Model Data). But even before standards were adopted, computer aided design processes had reduced the number of design hand-offs. In the long term, design quality improved and production costs were lowered, resulting in high quality products at a better price.

BPM is "CAD/CAM" for the IT Industry—the automa-tion of IT itself based on digital models of business processes. Using BPM, business processes will be created, discovered, de-signed and deployed more readily than ever before. Hundreds of variants will be generated and tested, now that the cost efficien-cies of BPM give designers the luxury of creating processes, the majority of which they will simply throw away as part of the creative and experimental processes. Compare this to today's long-winded and error-prone software development process.

Processes management will close the loop that links design, optimization and analysis. As this approach gains wide accep-tance, or as industry gorillas turn collaborative process design systems into de facto industry standards, the kind of business-to-business reengineering that James Champy defines under the brand "X-Engineering"[90] will become viable.

Because processes will be opened to computer-assisted refinement and transformation—just like 3-dimensional CAD/CAM product models are today—all processes will improve in quality along multiple dimensions: better, faster and less expensive. Even more significant, with the power and precision of computer-assisted design, business processes will be better fit for purpose: unique (competitive) and compelling (to customers). BPM provides a direct path from business process design to execution, turning companies, and their IT suppliers, into process manufacturers, not purveyors of commonly deployed solutions. Compare this with today's hyped-to-death, lowest common denominator, broad appeal, best practice, packaged software applications. Those IT services companies or end users that master BPM will share with their customers in the wealth, productivity gains, innovation and lowered costs that the industrial design and manufacturing industries have already experienced as a result of implementing a direct path from product design to realization.

Champy recognizes a significant business opportunity in this scenario. In a May 2002 article, he said, "If [companies] could improve the efficiency of these cross-organizational administrative processes by 50 percent, it would result in annual savings of $400 billion."[91] He cites the logistics industry as an example—the industry whose processes move goods from company to company or from company to consumer. Globally, companies spend about $2 trillion a year on logistics-related services, 40 percent of which is administrative costs, according to Champy.

Similar issues plague other industries. David Webber cites the healthcare industry, describing it as, "A disaster zone where information paralysis and old paper thinking still crushes service and availability. How can Carr conclude IT is finished already? There is so much waste it's not funny—and companies are paying for this in high hidden costs but do nothing about it. My list of areas not carrying their own weight includes taxation, accounting, healthcare, the legal system, education and training, insurance, investing, retirement planning, politics and access."[92]

Across all industry sectors, customers, suppliers and partners will need to collaborate on new process designs and logistics in order to scale down costs and prices. The technology of the 1990s was simply too expensive and complex to support open process collaboration in dynamic value chains. Proprietary Electronic Data Interchange (EDI) systems were complicated, expensive and rigid—oriented only to simplistic trade processes which fell far short of the richness and nuance inherent in truly collaborative inter-company, value-chain relationships. Traditional EDI, too, will be re-invented as a result of process management.

Boeing is a world-class example of this type of collaboration. The company designed its 777 airliner in cyberspace by electronically sharing its CAD/CAM design tools and processes with engineers, customers, maintenance personnel, project managers and component suppliers across the globe. No physical model. No paper blueprints. The nature of this process is captured in the slogan, "The 777 is a bunch of parts flying together in close formation." As a result, Boeing's customers no longer have to wait three years or more for a new airplane. Through process collaboration Boeing aims to deliver a plane in eight to 12 months, and the company expects to have the capacity to build 620 airplanes annually, up from 228 in 1992.

Therefore, when reading Carr's article, CEOs should take care to contrast his pessimistic views of IT with these possibilities—with IT of a different kind. BPM need not be applied on the scale of Boeing computer-aided methods, but the principles are the same. CEOs that recognize the potential of BPM will forge value chains where companies, their suppliers and trading partners "fly together in close formation," dominating their markets and delighting their customers.

To summarize:

- Over time, our definition of IT changes. The "I" in IT originally meant data.
- The "I" in IT is continuously re-defined as technology evolves, creating new commodity platforms. Today, the focus of IT is on business processes, and their management.

- The new "I" in IT is "P"—the business process—and companies are learning how to use the scale and ubiquity of Old IT to create new value, with their customers and partners.

A Catharsis of Sorts for the IT Industry

Each element of IT has been subject to its own commoditization trajectory. Nowhere is this more evident than what became known during the 1990s as the hunt for new Killer Apps, a desperate rush to develop and market packaged software designed to appeal to a broad market (the majority of companies) and delivered in the form of software, such as monolithic ERP, CRM and SCM packages, where the business processes were engrained. As research fellow Douglas Neal at Computer Sciences Corporation states "ERP [an example of packaged software] is as flexible as wet concrete before installation, and as flexible as dry concrete after installation."

"Jack of all trades, master of none" packaged software must take some of the blame for IT's bad press that contributed to the attention given to Carr's article. Will tech vendors learn from their mistakes? Today, the same vendors that created ERP are trying to create so-called cross apps, new packaged software that covers areas of IT automation unsupported by any existing software. One such area is PLM (product lifecycle management) that Michael Hammer described at US Process World, May 2003, as "yet another inappropriate attempt by the IT industry to package business processes."[93] Some have estimated the complexity and size of PLM, as a packaged application, to be six times that of ERP!

Given the scale of costs involved in ERP rollouts, mainly customization, one can hardly imagine the implications for companies rolling out PLM. Unless based on BPM, PLM as a packaged application is a non-starter. This requires packaged software providers to abandon building on the database system with its static data models, and build on the BPM system instead. Companies can (and some already have) start this process themselves by using new BPM systems to leverage their existing IT assets, just as two decades ago they applied shared database management systems long before ERP vendors took them up as the basis of their application suites.

To Carr's credit, he clearly prodded a nerve in the IT industry and says more about the IT industry, instead of providing any insight into how businesses gain strategic advantage through the integration of information processing elements in products and services. Some IT-industry reaction was not so much rebuttal, as it was a *catharsis*. Carr unlocked the door to a taboo that was stifling the IT industry's ability to discuss its own future.

Paul Andrews, writing in the Seattle Times confirms the tendency of the IT industry to avoid hard facts, "Rebuttals to Carr's comments have been predictably—and unfortunately—defensive. PC boosters [pointing to Microsoft and Intel] have focused on the industry's track record of innovation and self-regeneration over three decades ... Which side is right? While Carr's points were somewhat overstated, they did identify the core frustration behind the IT crisis. Innovation is happening, yes. But at this point, IT may be more in need of renovation. By renovation I mean, generally, fixing what's broke. IT's big challenge these days isn't getting more speed from its networks or finding better software or greater storage capacity. It's making things work."[94]

Microsoft's Gates acknowledges the problem, "We disagree with all of this [IT Doesn't Matter]. We fully acknowledge the harsh realities ... [but] there are solutions to every one of those things. People talk about total cost of ownership, and we decided we had to design out products to address those challenges ... The IT audience, developer, knowledge worker, the way business processes are done, the way people deal with information at home. With all those pieces in place, we've just started to scratch the surface [of] what software can enable."[95]

For the IT industry Carr is a two edged sword. While the industry will come under increased scrutiny from both businesses and venture capitalists, he does provide a catharsis of sorts. This was confirmed by Capital One CIO, Bailer, who stated that Mr. Carr had performed "a great service"[96] by stimulating debate about the role of information technology. Bailar went on to say that "the article's flaw was in discussing the maturity of information technology in terms of industrial technologies like railroads, steam and the telegraph." These, he noted, were "single-purpose technologies, whereas the computer is a programmable, general-purpose technology with all but infinite possibilities."

IT will indeed be viewed as a commodity, and correctly so, if IT providers continue to package business processes in software instead of providing effective process management tools that take the complexity out of process design and deployment. For as Carr says, reflecting on the type of process change enabled by IT automation in the past "... where we saw process change, all companies were making the same process change."[97] This is the consequence when companies procure the same software that is available to competitors, and where that software engrains the business process, creating a commodity, as opposed to being *process neutral* and providing the tools to manage the complete process lifecycle.

Unless IT developers can use BPM systems to re-energize the ability of business to differentiate their business processes, the world Carr paints may prove to be closer to the truth than even he believed when he wrote his article. Without BPM, companies will find themselves at the mercy of any company that deploys the same packaged software processes. With BPM the same company will be able to differentiate, yet simultaneously enjoy the advantages of a more standard, yet process-neutral, infrastructure.

Herein lies a paradox at the center of Carr's article, for BPM, while enhancing differentiation, at the same time creates new opportunities for further IT cost reduction and standardization. Does this mean "IT Doesn't Matter"? Not in the least, for as companies shift to a process-oriented infrastructure enabled by BPM, they open up new opportunities for innovation, and process-centric applications that aren't built on top of databases the way ERP is built today, but on top of the business process management system. With this BPM capability, companies will be able to analyze, manipulate, transform and optimize end-to-end business processes. This is the pattern of the next fifty years of business and IT.

Just as business people use their email systems to write their own email messages, business processes should be defined and owned by business users, not the IT department. By contrast, the traditional view is that an IT application *is* the business process, albeit engrained or embedded in packaged software. Casting this traditional view of business process ownership aside, BPM is moving the goal posts and changing the rules of the game, by digitizing processes, not just data. This allows the IT function to own the BPM systems, but not the processes deployed upon it and optimized by the business.

For years IT has automated the business; now it's time for the business to automate IT, taking traditional software development off the critical path of business change and innovation. BPM systems can manage many of the complexities inherent to today's software stack, allowing the business to focus purely on the specification of the business process, not IT artifacts. Today's BPM systems can provide straight-through process management, allowing business people to model, deploy and manage mission-critical business processes without the intervention of IT—just like businesspeople everywhere do with spreadsheets for numerical calculation or industrial designers do with CAD/CAM tools in manufacturing.

BPM systems include core tools for process modeling, analysis and simulation. Many such tools are already in use in companies today and are being linked to a mission-critical BPM foundation and platform. Even more powerful tools will emerge in the future, such as tools to support Mergers and Acquisitions or Value Chain Integration. Many companies in specific sectors will use BPM systems to create tools of their own, oriented to the specific strategic applications in their sector.

Process design will be *owned* by business people using the

BPM systems provisioned by IT, just as data models are owned by the business today. IT will have a lesser role in the process design, this being diffused throughout the business. On the other hand, IT practitioners with extensive backgrounds in general systems thinking will be able to rise above just supporting the BPM technology and on to helping business people with their process-oriented applications. Moreover, IT will be responsible for the new process-oriented applications that leverage the process designs the business deploys on the BPM system.

Myriad applications will be built on top of BPM systems, in the way they are today with database systems. BPM provides a birds-eye view of all processes in the enterprise. Process-oriented applications can manipulate whole processes directly, not just discrete components or data of a given functional application. With such systems, the *business process* supersedes the *computer application* as software's metaphor. For example, a company can define a digital Six Sigma *process* to improve other business processes, completely obviating the notion of a functional application as the primary means of packaging software.

Other immediate uses of BPM systems make for a long list: accountability, activity-based costing, activity-value analysis, business performance management, business process outsourcing, competitive intelligence, concurrent engineering, collaboration, cost-benefit analysis, crisis management, critical-path analysis, customer process alignment, decision management, economic value analysis (EVA), information management, interorganizational systems, just-in-time (JIT), key performance indicators, knowledge management, lean enterprise, lifetime customer value, management by objectives, mass customization, pay-for-performance, portfolio analysis, resource-based strategy, security audit, scenario planning, simulation, strategic alignment and planning, supply chain optimization and transparency. Even this list does not do justice to the many creative uses companies will find once they understand the significance of the shift from data digitization and data management systems, to process digitization and process management systems.

An Epilog to Data

Even if one accepts Carr's data-centric premises, we should not dismiss the value of data so readily. It did bring about great operational efficiencies through economies of scale. As 800-pound industry gorillas like Wal-Mart bear witness, hyper-operational efficiency itself can be a source of strategic advantage in dominating certain industries (goodbye mom-and-pop retailers.) But even using old IT, more classically defined strategic advantage was still available. Witness the advent of fault-tolerant data-handling computers that enabled a strategic breakthrough in banking—the ATM machine. By adopting ATM technology early, two innovators, Bank of America and Citibank, gained global dominance in retail banking and have helped sustained their lead, building sophisticated services delivered through the ATM networks.

Alinean Research also highlights the value of data technologies, stating that "from databases, for instance, has sprung the promise of truly individualized customer contact; from the rudiments of factory planning come supply chains that can shift production within days of changes in customer demand or of geopolitical turmoil."[98]

But is data enough? John Hagel refers to the "backlash sweeping through executive suites against IT spending." The current economy, outside of the IT sector, is not kind to either the IT industry or to the industry's innovators, as the very existence of Carr's article proves all too well. At the moment, most companies are completely unaware that anything but piecemeal applications, databases and systems integration solutions exist to meet new and changing business needs and few have the time, patience or R&D funds to find out. No wonder they judge that we have reached the end of the road for IT, for they are not looking!

Others remain gun-shy about recent breakthroughs in business process management that can go directly to the source of today's business and IT challenges, and fewer still have joined the ranks of the early adopters of business process technologies.

Some naysayers sound like an echo from 1899 when the head of the United States Patent Office, Charles Duell, was reported to have argued, falsely as it turns out, to close the Patent Office because "everything that could have been invented, has been invented."[99] Today, naysayers will wave Carr's article and proclaim that "here's proof that IT (and extrapolating on Carr's misconceptions, BPM) doesn't matter!"

Others believe that everything that can be invented has not yet been invented, and not all inventions are yet well understood, or even yet to be invented. Although business process management is inevitable, the road ahead for BPM will be as bumpy as any other innovation before it, and many have written about the difficulties of what consultant Geoffrey Moore calls crossing the chasm.

On the other hand, if the success of the last fifty years of data-oriented IT is anything to go by, crossing the chasm to the next fifty years of process-oriented IT will be something to behold. For as Harvard professor Warren McFarlan points out in his rebuttal to Carr, "it is naive to assume that other sharply discontinuous technologies will not offer similar transformation opportunities in the future … only the senior management team's imagination limits new IT-based opportunities."[100]

Rebutting the Rebuttals and Alternative Futures

In Carr's rebuttal to the rebuttals published in the June 2003 issue of *HBR* online, the month following the publication of his original article, he writes, "Let me restate the gist of my argument, which at times gets lost in the responses. As IT's core functions—data processing, storage and transmission—have become cheaper, more standardized, and more easily replicable, their ability to serve as the basis for competitive advantage has steadily eroded. … I find nothing in these letters [to the Editor] to contradict that argument."[101]

Carr seems to miss the points raised by his critics, for if we are to paraphrase them, they might have said "Mr. Carr, it's not that you are wrong in all details, only that the conclusions you reach and the recommendations you provide are ill-founded and unconvincing for they only account for the elephant's tail, not the whole elephant." But just for a moment let's take the counter view and assume that Carr really is correct—data processing, data storage and data transport (his definition of IT) are, indeed, commodities. One might respond, "So what?"

As journalist Mark Anderson said, "Whereas the HBR editor got it right in flagging the commoditization of some elements of IT—PCs, servers, data storage and packaged software—he erred by casting his net too widely, taking in elements of IT that resist commoditization. Worse, he was grievously, even dangerously wrong in his conclusion that IT no longer acts as a source of competitive differentiation among companies."[102] So what if some IT capabilities have joined the ranks of other commodity business services. Isn't that something that should be welcomed? Carr's thesis has cast further shadows and uncertainties over the information technology industry, at a time when, as Brian Arthur states "the economy is quiet now, gestating a new phase."[103]

Analyst Tom DeMarco at Cutter Consortium had similar misgivings about Carr's pessimistic advice to be a follower, not a leader, "There has to be an element of vision. That's the thing that can't be commoditized. ... He's saying, 'Don't be a visionary.' This is unhealthy, because some weak-minded but powerful person looking for something to cut will read Carr and say, 'Let's cut IT.' That's a shame. The view that IT doesn't matter is equivalent to the view that the printing press has had its run. But the printing press wasn't about printing enough Bibles for all the people. It was about creating a man whose knowledge is bigger than what lies in his head, and the impact of that has never peaked. I think that will be true of IT as well. Man is an information animal, and IT lies as close as anything to the core of his endeavors."[104]

In writing this book, we thought long and hard about our response. Could we be accused of being the opposite of Carr, making similar mistakes to those made during the dot-bomb era, selling 'next-tech BPM snake-oil' to prop up an ailing IT industry, or just finding an excuse to rail against Carr's arguments? In presenting the case for business process management as the real issue of IT and strategic advantage as an antidote to Carr, we don't believe we are falling into the trap of what Mark Anderson described, "the great hope of the IT industry is that the tech bubble of the late 1990s never really burst—it just deflated in the wake of massive over-investment and overbuild during the dot-com."[105] On the other hand, neither do we believe in quick fixes. There will be no quick re-bound of the IT sector for, as Edward Yardeni chief investment strategist at Prudential Securities says, "Right now there is a disconnect between the run-up in tech stocks and the technology spending expectations of CIOs."[106]

But, as is only natural, not everyone will agree with us about the significance of business process management to move the IT story forward, as the comments of Stephen Roach, Morgan Stanley's chief economist, make all too clear. "That's the debate. Is technology just another crummy factor of production dressed up in new clothes, or is it really an agent of continuing change in the way we do business and communicate? My view is that it is a modern-day version of a factor of production [like electricity]."[107] Perhaps, but, then again, perhaps not.

Like all true buildouts, as opposed to dot-bomb false starts, the focus now must be on hard work, reliability, industrial-strength end-to-end value-chain solutions, and the management of complexity, security and trust. At the heart of these endeavors will be the *business process*—the very crux of IT today.

Although Carr's timing is perfect for appealing to techno-phobic corporate cost cutters who want no more than sound bites to justify their actions, his conspicuous oversight of the crux of IT and his myopic analysis of the elephant's tail only serve as dangerous distractions for business leaders coping with the real and pressing needs of this very day. It's that red herring thing, again.

Doug Leone, a partner at Sequoia Capital one of the oldest VC firms in Silicon Valley, reports, "there has never been a

better time to start a company."[108] Leone points to "Valley rents
[being] the lowest they've been in nearly a decade, highly skilled
labor [being] plentiful, and venture capitalists still sitting on at
least five years worth of capital to invest (estimated by some to
be about $90 billion)." Small companies like Intalio and BEA are
challenging incumbents such as IBM and Microsoft and changing how business software and business processes are designed,
deployed and managed. In turn, Microsoft is investing $6.8
billion in R&D in FY '04.[109]

All this bodes well for businesses that want to reinvigorate
their performance and gain new sources of competitive advantage. Microsoft's Ballmer agrees, "We look out there like kids in
a candy store saying what a great world we live in ... Companies
need to focus on bringing value to customers ..."

Indeed, companies are looking for secrets, skills and tools
that will enable them to create and mesh together business processes that are so outstanding that customers will pay to use them
time and time again. We know of no more strategically effective
or operationally cost-efficient methods and techniques for
delivering compelling value to customers, at all touch points of
the business, than BPM.

What Should Companies Do?

The shift to BPM as a business practice and the shift from
applications to business processes as the epicenter of the software world can seem perplexing at first glance. To put business
process management to work for your organization, take several
small steps rather than one large, doomed-to-fail, step:

1. *Start with Business Metrics.* It all starts with *metrics,* for what
companies really want are measurable *results.* As Andrew Spanyi
explains, "This means increased revenues and higher earnings.
But while you can target improved results, you can't *manage* results. You can only manage the clusters of activities, *business processes,* that are most likely to produce the desired results. That's
why implementing BPM practices throughout the organization is
the best method by which organizations can produce the desired

results."[110] Because you cannot manage what you cannot measure, measure the performance of your business processes and how well they contribute to achieving strategy goals.

2. *Start with Business Processes, Not Technology.* Process pioneer Michael Hammer says companies that managed ERP in *process* terms were the successful ones, ones that didn't were not successful, and that's the whole point. "People started with the technology and then discovered it was a process issue. The pattern [CRM, PLM etc.] keeps repeating, which is depressing because it doesn't have to be that way."[111] Design new business processes from the outside in, starting with the customer and the customer's customer. Don't get distracted by package vendors' attempts to fit you into their commodity designs available to competitors.

3. *Start from the Top-Down, and from the Bottom-Up.* Hammer insists BPM is an entirely new way of thinking, "Most senior managers at organizations have a limited set of tools for improving performance," and he lists them. "There's financial management, organizational redesign, strategic refocusing, M&A, but the idea of using *processes* as the critical lever to improve performance is an up to the minute idea at most organizations. Our collective responsibility is to help organizations understand the power of that."[112]

The tipping point in business processes thinking must come from the top—from the commanding heights—from those who have the power to mandate change. But rather than mandating BPM, chief executives must themselves tightly link business strategy to business processes, for it is the business process that translates strategic thinking into execution.

If indeed what counts in business are results, the formula for business success has two variables: *excellent strategy* plus *execution*. Strategy defines the *what*, and because business processes are how work gets done, they are the *how* in execution.

Business process management is the most effective way of managing execution, as it both avoids the compromise of customization steps, time and costs involved with rigid functional applications and aligns the process directly to existing work practices. Functional application packages will always be, at best, a poor approximation of business strategy intent, for there is no direct link from strategy to deployed process, except via tedious customization of software and organizational change. By contrast, business processes are direct representations of strategy execution and there need be no step between process definition and process deployment.

To maintain the vital link between strategy and execution, members of the senior management leadership team must themselves "own" end-to-end business processes, those that cross the white space on the organization chart. Furthermore, because metrics apply to senior management as well as any other component of the business, executive rewards must be tied to the performance of those end-to-end business processes and the results they produce.

"It's a massive commitment for an organization in which measurements, rewards, cultures and careers will change," says Micheal Hammer. "Waving a wand won't get it done but there is, yes, a process that starts with the big boss. It involves identifying processes, appointing process owners, establishing metrics, picking processes to focus on, coming up with new designs, implementing in a phased approach, then putting in instrumentation and technology to support it. It's a kind of Planet of the Apes scenario where we are only just rediscovering our roots, where technology was a diversion. His new protagonist is the process owner, a senior executive charged by the CEO, backed to the hilt by top executives, and responsible for creating and insuring that a process is executed across an organization."[113] Here, Hammer speaks of the end-to-end business process that delivers ultimate value to customers, and this is what Micheal Porter calls primary activities in his value chain analysis. In addition, Porter describes support activities, those bottom-up business processes that can provide efficiencies in support of primary activities.

Only when senior management commits to an investment

that makes business process management *systemic,* bottom-up as well as top-down, can the process-managed enterprise emerge. That means investing in people and BPM technology platforms available to all—inside your company and across the value chain.

Even isolated support processes are a cause for concern. John Jainschigg, Editor in Chief of *Communications Convergence Magazine,* explains, "I think we need to re-acknowledge the primacy of the worker-as-contributor and cultivate a journeyman relationship between workers and their tools. In this process, we need to redefine individual job-descriptions, so that jobs are no longer considered in isolation from the computational (and other) innovations developed to do the work, and from the worker's resulting contributions towards the global improvement of corporate intelligence and best practice. Which simply means that, 'Okay, getting out the Annual Report on time and under budget is Job #1, but so is writing down the steps, describing the data sources, the processing, the output file formats, and all the other details of the job so that a year from now, the next drone sitting in my seat will find this a push-button procedure. Because if I don't do that, I will be fired, or at best, this will still be my job, next year.' My feeling is that process must be developed from the ground up, and that—contrary to Carr's thesis—IT matters very much ... And will matter more when we're all tasked with being our own CIOs, and obsolescing ourselves as we proceed up the ladder of promotion. In selected instances, this kind of thing has already happened—conversion to desktop publishing, for example, was a process largely driven by the articulate demands of impatient freelancers for better tools. It would be nice to see other business processes 'owned' by their executors and subjected to similar fast-track evolution. Nice fantasy, eh? Meanwhile, my assistant is still using Excel to build flat-file databases and normalizing address information by hand ... this may take a while." [114]

Dr. Barbara Belon, a Director at Norwalk College brings personal experience to bear with regard to bottom-up processes, "All one has to do is think of their last painful business experience and they can see the need for BPM. For me, it was having to track down an invoice and purchase requisition, which I had duly processed to pay a very good vendor of mine, only to receive a phone call asking why they hadn't been paid. The business process had broken down somewhere in the accounts payable office, which sat on the payment request because they had never received the signoff from Receiving (product came directly to me, not through Receiving, hence the problem ... but no one ever told me that I needed to let them know that the product had been received). If we had a fully functional business process for handling anything the college purchased, this kind of stuff wouldn't happen. Technology would enable me to check on the payment status, view any 'holds,' and be notified when actions were taken. My vendor wouldn't have been aggravated and our relationship bruised. I wouldn't have had to waste time tracking down work that I had already completed. Of course, this is just one process in the mountain of processes that needs attention and distracts me and others in the College's leadership team from our real work. Thank goodness for 'commodity' IT solutions because no one IT staff is going to have the time to create everything from scratch to support the business process framework."[115] Belon is, as most executives are, often drained by having to devote energies to working around broken processes instead of applying those energies to strategic activities.

Multiply Jainschigg's annual report scenario and Belon's patching relationships with unpaid vendors by the hundreds and even thousands of business processes in a single company and then again by the six million firms in the U.S. and the opportunities for performance improvements in individual companies and the economy as a whole are astounding.

Top management must invest in people and BPM platforms that provide the capabilities to fully manage both strategic, top-down and operational, bottom-up business processes.

4. *Approach BPM as an "Incremental rEvolution," not a Big Bang, Killer App.* The good news about business process management solutions is that they are not big bang, all or nothing

investments—those days are long gone. Business process management doesn't displace what you already have, it leverages your current business and IT assets without duplicating resources or disrupting the value they contribute to customers. Business process management represents a heritage-friendly, "legacy" free, approach where investment and payback proceed one business process at a time, avoiding the enterprise upheaval characteristic of ERP and CRM installations of the past.

Yes, companies will need business process management platforms and systems, but unlike big-bang, disruptive ERP and CRM systems, the key to business process management is *do no harm*, that is, don't disrupt your company. Instead, establish a BPM greenhouse and grow your capabilities and resources at a pace that won't disrupt your company, but will bring tangible results from the get-go. Start by applying BPM to end-to-end business processes that you know are either broken, or missing. Make the investment in technology and people so that employees at all levels can take command of the business processes that they are directly involved with and responsible for their performance. In short, approach BPM as the business rEvolution that it is.

5. *Get Your Own House In Order, and then Grow Incrementally.* Before collaborating with your trading partners and customers, get your house in order by first collaborating between your primary functional activities. The key word here is collaboration, not consolidating these functions into rigid ERP or CRM application packages characterized by unacceptable costs. With this first, internal-collaboration step accomplished, extend your collaboration to trading partners and customers using an incremental approach that is always tied to current company strategy and initiatives. The days of the monolithic ERP and CRM applications are over. Start with your customer strategy, and then realign your customer-oriented business processes to fit the strategy—that's the humble secret to successful business process management, the secret to successful business relationships, and the secret to successful business.

6. *Avoid the Major Pitfalls.* The major pitfalls in transitioning to a process-managed enterprise are many, as business people naturally cling to preconceived notions. These pitfalls include:

- Failure to understand that IT can be used for more than automation, that it can cover the business process lifecycle and provide tools for any process, manual or automated. BPM is about managing the organization's "white space," not just automated IT processes coded into software.
- Failure to understand that BPM can separate the engine from the process, allowing companies to differentiate, completely and utterly.
- Failure to understand that BPM proponents are not saying that IT is the answer, but that people without tools are not going to cut it in today's hyper-competitive value chains.
- Failure of executive management to own end-to-end business processes, for as Hammer says, the new "protagonist is the process owner, a senior executive charged by the CEO, backed to the hilt by top executives, and responsible for creating and insuring that a process is executed across an organization."[116]
- Failure of executive management to instill business process thinking, as Spanyi puts it, "from the board room to the lunch room," and failure to make the investment in people and technology that translates thinking into doing.

The 90-Day Plan

Because business process management is new—it is not another killer app or a fashionable management theory—there is no standard, cookie-cutter approach to adopting it. Indeed, if there was, business leaders would be rightly skeptical of its value, just as they have become skeptical of the promises of packaged software vendors.

The emphasis for the first three months should therefore be on learning and experimentation. Here we present one possible scenario when executive management decides to lead a process-managed enterprise. Our experience, however, is that today, BPM is growing organically, driven by the vision of senior business and technology architects and CIOs (the very ones that Carr wants to stand down) rather than top-down dictates. The foremost challenge then is to instill business process thinking in all the thinkers, actors and doers that lead your company—as Spanyi says, "from the board room to the lunch room."

First month: From innocence to awareness

Involve business and systems analysts in comparing BPM to existing methods and systems, focusing on the new process-modeling and process-deployment techniques. Identify relevant BPM technologies, architectures and methods. List all existing internal projects that aim to improve processes, their associated IT systems and technical activities, and costs. Develop an analysis framework to compare a piecemeal approach with the continuous approach of BPM. Identify possible targets for pilot projects, noting the process domain and related IT systems involved.

Second month: From apprentice to practitioner

Develop an outline for a management perspective on BPM in the context of existing strategies. Brainstorm BPM's organizational implications. Define in more detail BPM's precise relationship to existing business and technology initiatives, such as enterprise integration and ERP, and to existing management initiatives, like Six Sigma, activity-based costing and value-chain analysis. Bring BPM technology into your domain and integrate it with a small core of applications at the heart of your process-improvement activities. Select one business domain for piloting BPM, focusing on a large, complex problem that so far hasn't been solved. While the initiative will probably take many months, the idea is to get started on a business-critical process rather than some trivial or contrived pilot. Use the test bed to demonstrate the radical nature and benefits of the BPM approach to executive management.

Third month: Epiphany

Use a process model to encode a part of your existing business strategy and to develop a process pattern that can be adopted across the company as a test. Identify the reasons others in your company will inevitably put forward to show the BPM approach "can't possibly work." Draft a plan that compares the total cost of process ownership "as is" with that of the BPM approach. Draft a detailed comparison between BPM and existing technologies and approaches. Complete the integration of operational systems for the chosen process domain to the process-management environment. Experiment with the redesign, deployment, execution, operations and analysis of variant process designs. Understand the trade-offs that BPM requires in order to reap its benefits.

The Fifty-Year Plan

BPM isn't a sprint, it's a way of life, and its intensity is governed by business priorities, not IT peddlers inside or outside the firm. BPM isn't the next big-bang killer app installed in order to compete with and emulate competitors; it's a platform to launch an incremental business rEvolution, one (carefully selected) end-to-end business process at a time.

The first fifty years of business automation have been about data processing and economies of scale. The second fifty years are all about competing for the future with the business process innovation and management. Does IT matter for the next fifty years? We think so.

But, then again, what if we revisit this issue in 2053? Perhaps the headlines of the May 2053 issue of HBR will be, "BPM Doesn't Matter," for at that time Bob Lewis' characterization that "business processes and practices have reached optimization nirvana" may just have happened. Companies would then fully and optimally serve their customers, "Earnings Won't Matter," and humans will answer to a higher calling as their raison d'être, for "Work Won't Matter."

Meanwhile, companies have a lot of work to accomplish

this very day, laying the foundation for the process-managed enterprise, and they cannot afford to be distracted by anyone shouting that IT doesn't matter.

Postscript on the Economy

At the beginning of this book, we talked about dangerous articles, and indeed while we were in the process of finishing this work, others were beginning to echo our concern. Law professors David Post and Bradford Brown linked "IT Doesn't Matter" directly to the economy, "[Carr] sounds like a basketball coach with a two point lead who tells his team to play the 'four corners'. It's a message of caution."[117] They point out that caution can be self-fulfilling and that "state of mind has a lot to do with how people and markets react. ... As Alan Greenspan said: "... we need to remain mindful of the possibility that lingering business caution could be an impediment to improved economic performance."[118]

Sen. John Edwards recently spoke to technology executives in northern Virginia. The Washington Post headlined its story about the speech, "Edwards Brings Revival Message to N. Va.; Presidential Hopeful Pledges New Opportunities For Dot-Com Industry." What was important wasn't so much what Edwards said but the fact that he recognized there's an opportunity in the tech sector for a candidate who wants to try and take the dialogue in another direction. That's what the sector needs, fervor to return to the hunt for the next "New New Thing."

Meanwhile, other voices also began to express concerns about the impact of the "IT Doesn't Matter" meme[119], including consultant George Schuseel who said, "I'm worried. We are in the middle of the worst recession in the history of data processing. And since I started programming on machines such as the UNIVAC I, Bendix G20 and IBM 7090, I can claim to have been around for the entire history of IT. Leading companies such as Sun and Oracle have lost more than 75 percent of their market value, and the situation is even worse for smaller companies: Many have gone out of business. As for venture-capital-funded startups, many never even came into existence in the first place."[120]

While Schussel was confident the recession would end, he expressed concern about the possibility of lasting damage. "IT budgets have been cut to a dangerous level. Companies are spending less on hardware, software and services. Thus, vendors have less income to invest in research and development and will reduce the number of innovative products they introduce. ... Then there are cuts in vendors' marketing budgets. Less advertising, smaller conferences, fewer market experts—all in all, much less information gets exchanged." It's unfortunate that the "IT Doesn't Matter" article can now be misused by technology-challenged business leaders to make Schuseel's worry a self-fulfilling prophecy.

It doesn't stop there, for the IT industry isn't an economic engine for its sector alone, it's a major driver of the economy as a whole. On July 8, 2003, the Wall Street Journal reported that, "During the past 2 1/2 years, the U.S. economy has lost more than three million private-sector jobs. Unfortunately for anyone hunting for work, that figure includes thousands of recruiters."

While there is no doubt that the economy is in a slump, it should be remembered that America's only real competitive edge is technology-enabled *innovation*, for smokestack industries and agriculture have long since been commoditized by globalization. But that doesn't mean propping up the IT industry in the way governments have propped up agriculture through subsidies. Quite the contrary. Santa Fe Institute's Brian Arthur elaborates in an interview with *CIO* magazine's Richard Pastore, "This country's one and only economic driver for the next several decades rests solely in the hands of CIOs. But Arthur isn't talking about CIOs shelling out more cash for additional servers, pumping new revenue into Silicon Valley. It's far more profound than that."[121]

"Arthur postulates that as industries encounter digital technologies, they are being fundamentally and organically transformed ... The effect will be previously undreamed-of processes and functionality that will alter what companies do, fundamentally transforming their industries. ...The encounters become the economic engine of growth. I don't see the driver coming from anywhere else. I don't see an enormous pent-up consumer demand, or the discovery of a vast new market (with the possible exception of China)—the traditional ways in which an economy would have expanded 150 years ago. I don't see any other source that will provide deep growth for the next several decades."[122]

Unlike Carr who says, "I think there's less of a need for those types of individuals [CIOs]," Arthur, an economist, believes that the major engine of growth for the economy will be in the hands of IT practitioners. "There's no other corporate officer who can see how to do this. If you're trained as an MBA, or a lawyer or a middle manager, you can't be expected to have the imagination to see what's possible—it's too complex. So I think it's going to be IT people showing top management what is possible."[123]

Indiana University's, Brad Wheeler confirms, "In my experience of working with senior business leaders in 26 countries, the cause of under performing IT spending is most frequently senior executives' failure to personally understand the role of information systems and to work effectively with their (revolving door) CIO. Carr's 'New Rules' further exacerbate this problem by setting firms up for a widening gap between their own IT capabilities and the continuing evolution of IT—does this sound familiar?"[124]

Lockheed's Ajit Kapoor wrote, "I was shocked when I read the article and thought that HBR was taking its cue from one of the British tabloids—I guess they needed a sensation."[125] Had the article been published in a lesser publication, and not in HBR, we doubt it would have received so much attention. It was the prestige of the *Harvard Business Review* that has given the piece an enhanced status and has led to its increased attention and commentary. We hope this book has expanded the argument and given the reader further information, breath and depth the subject deserves, for it is a vital subject, not just for corporate cost-cutters, but for the business leaders who must move the economy forward. They are grappling with the full scope of IT issues, not just deciding whether to follow others and to cut out unnecessary PC upgrades.

The impact the debate has created may also extend into the field of education. Schussel is already concerned that enrollment in IT and e-business-related courses has plummeted to less than one-third its level in 2000 according to his contacts at schools such as Wharton, MIT, Carnegie Mellon and Cornell. Indeed, we share this concern and pointed to it in an *Internet World* article entitled "The New M.B.A Curriculum." Now is the time for business schools to provide their graduates with business process management knowledge and hands-on skills needed in the process-managed enterprise to drive innovation. The future will be owned by those who don't just improve processes, but who create methods and systems that automate their creation, not just their function, to achieve competitive advantage.

One institution taking up this theme is Boston University's school of Management. Chairman of the IS Department, Venkat Venkatraman stated in a compelling article in *InformationWeek* that "At Boston University School of Management, we have embarked on a new bold vision: to educate a select set of students to be proficient at the intersection of business and IT. Our belief is that the business world needs more managers who are comfortable straddling the domains of business and technology in ways to build the necessary bridges. What we have found lacking today are managers who are truly cross-domain experts, who don't shy away from understanding the technological issues in sufficient ways to examine possible future scenarios of value creation. The problem stems from a historical reliance on separating IT as a technical, specialist field, not as part of the mainstream business agenda. Such a separation is no longer true and, indeed, is counterproductive. We are training these future managers with a fundamental belief that IT matters but in ways different from the past."[126]

We agree with his continued assessment that, "It's clear that we are in a major transition in global business operations, and IT is a big part of it. Computing has become faster and cheaper, and we're able to digitize many products in ways that couldn't have been dreamt about a decade ago. ... IT is integral to many products. More products are becoming digital. Microprocessors are becoming smaller and cheaper, and we are able to put the power of computing into everyday products and packages. The automobile is a computer on wheels. In a typical car today, the cost of computing is more than the cost of rubber or steel. The cellular phone morphs into a digital camera and a music player and a PDA. Sony's success in the next decade will depend on its ability to master the intricacies of digital technology across its wide array of products. IT shapes the next-generation business processes. For Wal-Mart, the current driver of competitive advantage is IT-enabled logistics and superior visibility of inventory. Its future driver of advantage is based on enhancing the efficiency and effectiveness of the supply chain using powerful radio-frequency identification tags with precise information throughout the logistics chain."

Venkatraman is correct that the management approach in business or academe to incorporating and embracing IT is not well understood. "The perennial list of questions continues—is it a cost center? Is it a service center? How much should we invest in IT? When should we invest? What's a relevant benchmark? What guidelines do we have to master this technological evolution? ... The management challenge is to ... analyze the possibilities, invest in the capabilities, and create new business models that are forward-looking. It's not about prediction but about staking out the building blocks of the future business landscape."

As the Great One, hockey superstar Wayne Gretsky once said, "I don't skate to where the puck is. I skate to where the puck is going to be." We hope this book has contributed to the debate about where the IT puck is going to be.

Appendix: A Recap of the Early Rebuttals Appearing in the Press

As far as we know, the first coverage in the press of "IT Doesn't Matter" was in a major article on the IT industry by Steve Lohr in the *New York Times* on Sunday, May 4, 2003. The article was reprinted on May 5 in the *International Herald Tribune.* Following this, a series of articles appeared in various business and technology titles. We applaud these journalists and analysts for their contribution to the debate. With its sensational head-line, provocative ideas and timing, more stories about "IT Doesn't Matter" will no doubt appear in due course and the legacy of this article will unfold for some time to come.

It is also without doubt that the debate over the strategic value of IT will continue in the *Harvard Business Review* and throughout the business world, now and into the future. For additional sources referenced in this work, we direct readers to the June 2003 online edition of HBR in which several of Carr's critics published *Letters To The Editor,* including John Seely Brown, John Hagel III, F. Warren McFarlan, Richard L. Nolan, Paul A. Strassmann, Marianne Broadbent, Mark McDonald, Richard Hunter, Bruce Skaiskis, Vladimir Zwass, Mark S. Lewis, Tom Pisello, Roy L. Pike, Vijay Gurbaxani, Steven Alter, Cathy Hyatt and Chris Schlueter Langdon. In the same issue, Carr responded to his critics with a *"Reply from Nicholas G. Carr."* He also lists many additional responses to his article at his Web site, http://www.nicholasgcarr.com.

We will also be happy to continue the dialog with you by sharing new information that comes to light after we go to print, at http://www.bpm3.com. For the record, here are some of the first stories and rebuttals to appear.

Paul Strassmann

Years before Carr's article, industry veteran and luminary, Paul Strassmann, had conducted research[127] that showed only a random correlation between IT spending per employee and return on shareholder equity, and concluded that spending money on information technology guarantees nothing.

More recently, Alinean Research published findings that confirm no consistent correlation between IT spending and financial performance, but which shed new light on why some companies come out ahead, and others come out short, even when they spend the same amount on IT. Why then would Strassmann, whose research seems superficially to validate Carr's thesis, feel so distressed that he felt the need to immediately send HBR a six-page critique?[128]

Strassman states that Carr "bases his conclusions entirely on his reasoning, by analogy, that IT must follow the same patterns that arose as businesses adopted steam engines, railroads, telephones, electric generators, and internal combustion motors. But any proof that rests entirely on analogies is flawed. This technique was used to uphold medieval dogma, and it delayed the advancement of science by centuries."

Tom Pisello, CEO and founder of Alinean Corporation, a research firm where Strassmann holds a board position, puts it this way, "Two companies investing the same amounts in identical technologies will yield vastly different results. What does this mean? What a company invests in, and how well it is applied to improve business practices, counts far more than how much is spent ... That's because every organization has unique needs and priorities."[129]

ComputerWorld

Frank Hayes, writing in *ComputerWorld*,[130] started to shed light on the matter, pointing out that, "Carr is right about one thing: You can't get sustainable competitive advantage by buying IT products and services. ... You get it with processes, skills and execution—the same things that let any business differentiate itself in ways that don't involve IT. ... But hey—that's not news! Every experienced IT (and MIS and data processing) manager over the past 40 years has doped this out." He points out that Nordstrom differentiates itself from Wal-Mart through its business processes, its employees' skills and how those employees execute on those processes. And Wal-Mart differentiates itself with its own business processes. "When IT is used most effectively, when it's really focused on the business it serves, it reinforces and amplifies that differentiation. ... It helps Wal-Mart be Wal-Mart and Nordstrom be Nordstrom. ... If that sounds a little fuzzy, it's because every company is unique ... And when that's what IT delivers, IT really does matter."

Fortune Magazine

David Kirkpatrick, writing in *Fortune Magazine*,[131] referred to by one journalist as "the poster-child for the anti-Carr movement," stated that Carr simply "misunderstands what information technology is." His interpretation of Carr's mistake is that "Carr thinks IT is merely a bunch of networks and computers" and highlights the article's complete disregard for the centrality of software.

Any human knowledge or information can be mediated and managed by software, a point picked up by Microsoft and PricewaterhouseCoopers in the same article, "The hardware, the stuff everybody's fascinated with, isn't worth a damn ... it's just disposable. Information technology is a knowledge capital issue. It's basically a large amount of human capital and software."

Their conclusion in our words: Carr failed to place sufficient emphasis on the "I" in "IT." The point was confirmed by the CIO of FedEx who declared himself "stunned" by Carr's article, and, as Microsoft pointed out, to say that IT doesn't matter is tantamount to saying that companies have enough information about their operations, customers, and employees. Ridiculous. Most CIOs report that companies are drowning in data, but starved of information. Based on this analysis Kirkpatrick went on to assert that Carr's article was "a sloppy mix of ersatz history, conventional wisdom, moderate insight and unsupportable assertion ... and dangerously wrong."

CNN/Money

Expanding on the growing debate and the "I" in IT, Adam Lashinsky writing for *CNN/Money*,[132] correctly identified that there may be two, yet to be precisely defined, elements in the story, stating, "As in any good intellectual debate, both writers make good points. Carr is accurately describing the technology world in the post-bubble era. Kirkpatrick proves that innovation isn't over yet."

InformationWeek

Bob Evans, writing in *InformationWeek*,[133] tried to move the Carr debacle on urging, "Where the article should have gone, I think, is outside the realm of embedded infrastructure and applications and into some attempts to look at what the future might look like. Instead, it assumes that the futures that befell railroads and steam engines will, inexorably and inevitably, be the future of IT. And I think that's astonishingly shortsighted."

Bob Evans gets even closer to the truth in a later article in *InformationWeek*,[134] inviting Ralph Szygenda, CIO of General Motors to comment. "Nicholas Carr may ultimately be correct when he says IT doesn't matter," Szygenda began. "But business-process improvement, competitive advantage, optimization, and business success, do matter and they aren't commodities ... precision investment on core infrastructure and process differentiation IT systems is called for." The GM CIO went on to point out that, "Yes, IT has elements of commoditization. PCs, telecommunications, software components such as payroll, benefit programs, business-process outsourcing, and maybe even operating systems and database-management systems are examples. But the application of information systems in a corporation's product design, development, distribution, customer understanding is probably at the fifth-grade level."

In another article in *Information Week,* this time by Rick Whiting,[135] General Motors CTO Tony Scott pointed out that, "Even technology that's a commodity still provides business flexibility." To put that another way, IT can be used to support, and manage, a company's own differentiated business processes. In the same article, CIO and executive VP Michael Harte at PNC Financial Services Group was quoted as saying that, "If anything, IT is becoming more productive with generations of IT portfolio-management tools."

Computerworld

Patricia Keefe writing for *Computerworld*[136] started to pick up on this theme, pointing out that unlike Carr she does not think IT has to dissolve into an entity that is strictly focused on maintenance, risk avoidance and cost-cutting for as she says, "Astute CIOs are already practicing this in some form or another." She goes much further writing that "Technology has the potential to succeed in permeating almost every aspect of our lives and the products we use. Some might say that creating all that new stuff won't be IT's job. The R&D, manufacturing and design groups will be responsible for weaving technology advances into consumer goods."

And on the same day in the same publication, Kathleen Melymuka presented an interview with Carr[137] in which he said, "I'm defining IT as the processing, storage and transmission of data, so I'm taking that quite broadly. ... As a means of differentiation, I think we're already past the peak and on the downside. ... The almost infinite scalability of many IT functions, combined with the rush to technical standardization, means there's no economic benefit to having proprietary applications ... All companies will be able to buy the capability, so no company will get advantage. ... I think there is still a danger of managers getting excited about the potential for advantage and moving too quickly into new technology."

Not wanting to let Carr off the hook, Kathleen went to construct the illusion of a roundtable discussion between Rob Austin and Andrew McAfee, both assistant professors of technology and operations management at Harvard Business School; Paul A. Strassmann, an IT management consultant, a Computerworld columnist and recently the acting CIO at

NASA; and Tom DeMarco, a Cutter Consortium analyst. They made the case for why IT matters more than ever.

In the virtual roundtable, Strassmann said, "When Wal-Mart started 40 years ago, anybody could have gone to NCR and bought the Teradata system, which is really the basis of Wal-Mart's success. The fact that you buy identical technology doesn't buy you anything. It's how you manage it. ... Let's go back to fundamental economics. The financial assets CFOs report on account for less than a third of the value of a corporation. Two-thirds of the valuation is based on knowledge capital, which is information. The CIO of the future will be responsible for the custody and protection and security of knowledge capital. Right now only the CFO has to sign a financial statement. I predict within 10 years the CIO will have to sign for the security of knowledge assets. Right now only the CFO can go to jail. My hope is for the CIO of the future to be also eligible to go to jail."[138]

EETimes

Richard Wallace writing in *EETimes*,[139] also fired back against Carr, quoting Intel's CEO Craig Barrett. "All of those common infrastructures and infrastructure elements that allow you to make or move material; they don't allow you to put intellectual content or value into what you are doing." Barrett went on to say that "economies today are measured in terms of the intellectual content that embedded in the products they sell." He could have gone further.

Bill Gates, in a CEO Summit at Redmond in May 2003 said, "Well, our view on this [HBR article] is that IT long ago moved away from being simply about back-office activities, simply about printing checks and keeping the account books. And, over these last seven years, it's moved to become the tool that determines whether your information workers can do their job effectively. Do they know what's going on with customer satisfaction? Are they engineering new models in a very effective way? Are they finding partners to work with in a strong fashion?

... Microsoft's view on this has been pretty constant throughout. When it [IT] became over-hyped, we were a little concerned about the promises that were being made during those times. At this stage, in a sense, you could say it's almost under-hyped."

USA Today

Kevin Maney, writing in *USA Today*,[140] highlighted such trends when he reported that Wall Street analysts, most prominently Steve Milunovich of Merrill Lynch talk of "bifurcation" of the IT market itself, into Dell at the low-priced commodity end and IBM at the high end, with every other computer company caught in a profit-draining no man's land. A similar stratification of commodity and high value products and services occurs in every other industry. Where Dell focuses its process differentiation on delivery excellence, customer service and build to order, rather than product innovation, IBM pumps billions of dollars a year into its massive scientific research labs and product innovation.

Gartner

Gartner's analysis[141] of "IT Doesn't Matter" brought us back to earth, simply by pointing out that where Carr goes wrong is "by equating IT with hardware and networks; rather, the essence of IT is information. Successful firms will use information and IT intelligently and in new ways to solve business problems and create customer value."

John Hagel

As respected writer John Hagel said in his rebuff to Carr at his Weblog,[142] "Extracting business value from IT requires innovations in business practices [processes]. In many respects, we believe Carr attacks a red herring—few people would argue that IT alone provides any significant business value or strategic advantage. Carr's article is dangerous because it endorses the growing view that IT offers only limited potential for strategic differentiation." Hagel expounds that in contrast to IT, previous technology innovations, such as railroads, began to stabilize and commodities as a dominant architecture emerged. We agree with Hagel in his assertion that "we have yet to see a dominant architecture for IT emerge." It's simply far too early.

Hagel points to the growth in distributed service architectures [Web services] as having the potential to create a virtuous circle when coupled to strategy development [sound like BPM?] and, that, far from believing that the potential for strategic differentiation through IT is diminishing Hagel says "the potential is increasing." Gartner agrees, stating, "Carr is wrong when he contends that IT innovation is winding down. Innovation through electronically enabled services, processes and products has only just begun."

We agree, but we also believe that the distributed computing system that IBM and Microsoft have already hyped to death (Web services) and which Hagel views as significant, is in fact nothing more than the *new* IT commodity, replacing existing commodity operating systems, databases and application servers. When commodity meets innovation, strategic value is generated. Amazon certainly used a once new commodity, the free and ubiquitous Internet, to wrest strategic advantage when the same commodity was available to established players who failed to see its value in the retail book industry. Today, many companies are struggling to see the value of Web services ... that is until they use a business process management system.

Hagel, together with John Seely Brown, former chief scientist at Xerox, went on to respond to Carr in an extended article published in the June 2003 of HBR. The article contained undertones of a warning to the IT industry, "If we've learned one thing from the 1990s, it's that big bang, IT-driven initiatives rarely produce expected returns. ... Rather than help companies understand that IT is only a tool, technology vendors have tended to present it as a panacea. 'Buy this technology and all your problems will be solved.'" Incumbent vendors of ERP, and new vendors of BPM systems, take note of Hagel and Brown's message.

Infoworld

Chad Dickerson, CTO of *Infoworld* eventually took the issue straight to the gut, "While I agree that what Carr defines as IT (the technologies used for processing, storing, and transporting information in digital form) is a commodity, I think his definition is too narrow and views IT within a sterile vacuum. It's still not easy to put it all together and make it work because the successful assembly of IT 'commodity inputs' is not a commodity itself. Think of IT like the food that comes into a restaurant— yes, the meat and vegetables most restaurants use are commodities that anyone can buy themselves, but what the restaurant does with the food is what really matters."[143] The real difference is the quality of the business process when it comes to sizzle, and when it comes to competitive advantage.

References

[1] Taschek, John, "IT does matter," *eWEEK,* July 14, 2003.

[2] Stewart, A. T., Introduction to "Does IT Matter? An HBR *Debate,"* Harvard Business Review, June 2003.

[3] http://www.alinean.com/HBR_PS.asp

[4] Bill Gates, Chairman and Chief Software Architect, Microsoft Corporation, remarks at the CEO Summit 2003, Redmond, Washington.

[5] Whiting, R., "CIOs Sure Think IT Matters," *InformationWeek,* May 23, 2003.

[6] Gurbaxani, V., Letter to the Editor, in "Does IT Matter? An HBR Debate," Harvard Business Review, June, 2003.

[7] Lohr, S., "Is technology business still a growth industry?," New York Times, May, 2003, reporting remarks by Intel to analysts.

[8] John Hagel's Weblog, http://www.johnhagel.com/blog20030515.html

[9] Email to the authors from Rajiv Gupta, June 2003.

[10] George F. Colony, "Forrester CEO looks above IT iceberg waterline", Forrester Research, June 2003.

[11] http://weblog.infoworld.com/dickerson/2003/06/02.html

[12] Kirkpatrick, D., "Stupid-Journal Alert; Why HBR's View of Tech Is Dangerous," *FORTUNE,* May 27, 2003.

[13] McFarlan, W., Nolan, R., Letter to the Editor, in "Does IT Matter? An HBR Debate," *Harvard Business Review,* June 2003.

[14] Lewis, S. M., Letter to the Editor, in "Does IT Matter? An HBR Debate," *Harvard Business Review,* June 2003.

[15] http://www.infoworld.com/article/03/07/24/HNballmerfam_1.html

[16] Alter, S., Letter to the Editor, in "Does IT Matter? An HBR Debate," *Harvard Business Review,* June 2003.

[17] Carr, Nicholas G., "IT Doesn't Matter," *Harvard Business Review,* May 2003.

[18] Evans, B., "Business Technology: IT Doesn't Matter?," *InformationWeek,* May 12, 2003.

[19] Waite, Steve, "Digitization GE Style," *Canadian Hedge Watch Newsletter,* May 7, 2001.

[20] http://newsroom.cisco.com/dlls/hd_062503.html

[21] Editor's introduction to "Does IT Matter? An HBR Debate," *Harvard Business Review,* June 2003.

[22] http://www.nicholasgcarr.com/articles/matter.html

[23] Melymuka, K., "Get Over Yourself: The Pervasiveness of IT may be making it strategically irrelevant," *Computerworld,* May 12, 2003.

[24] http://www.issurvivor.com/

[25] Email to the authors from Gillian Taylor, July 2003.

[26] Theoretical foundations of mobile distributed processes and the Pi Calculus, Robin Milner, Professor of Computer Science, Cambridge University,

UK, and ACM Turing Award Winner.

[27] The Business Process Management Initiative (BPMI.org)

[28] Fingar P., Smith H., *Business Process Management: The Third Wave,* Meghan-Kiffer Press, 2003, http://www.bpm3.com

[29] Sinur J., Thompson, J., "The Business Process Management Scenario: Strategy, Trends and Tactics," Gartner, June 2003.

[30] Strassmann, P., Letter to the Editor, in "Does IT Matter? An HBR Debate," *Harvard Business Review,* June 2003.

[31] Lewis, M., Letter to the Editor, in "Does IT Matter? An HBR Debate," *Harvard Business Review,* June 2003.

[32] "Fair Exchange," Thursday June 12, 2003, *The Guardian.*

[33] *ibid.*

[34] Gurbaxani, V., Letter to the Editor, part of "Does IT Matter? An HBR Debate," Harvard Business Review, June, 2003.

[35] Ticoll, David, "In writing off IT, you write off innovation," *Globe and Mail Update,* Thursday, May. 29, 2003.

[36] Anderson, M., "Article of Faith," *The Ottawa Citizen,* June 26, 2003.

[37] Strassmann, P., Letter to the Editor, part of "Does IT Matter? An HBR Debate," *Harvard Business Review,* June 2003.

[38] http://www-1.ibm.com/grid/about_grid/what_is.shtml

[39] Carr, Nicholas G., "IT Doesn't Matter," *Harvard Business Review,* May 2003.

[40] Anderson, M., "Article of Faith," *The Ottawa Citizen,* June 26, 2003.

[41] Andrews, P., "IT does matter; fixing it might just convince us," *Seattle Times,* June 23 2003.

[42] Davenport, H. T., Prusak, L., *What's the Big Idea?,* Harvard Business School Press, 2003.

[43] Email to the authors from Ajit Kapoor, June 2003.

[44] Anderson, M., "Article of Faith," *The Ottawa Citizen,* June 26, 2003.

[45] *ibid.*

[46] Lohr, S., "The Tech Rebound That Isn't Quite," *New York Times,* June 23, 2003.

[47] "Is the Information Revolution Dead?," W. Brian Arthur, *Business 2.0,* March 2002.

[48] Smith, H., Fingar, P., From the Introduction to *Business Process Management: The Third Wave,* Meghan-Kiffer Press, 2003, http://www.bpm3.com

[49] Strassmann, P., Letter to the Editor, part of "Does IT Matter? An HBR Debate," *Harvard Business Review,* June 2003.

[50] Reply from Nicholas G. Carr, in "An HBR Debate—Does IT Matter," *Harvard Business Review,* June 2003.

[51] http://www.simulconference.com/clients/sowf/dispatches/dispatch2.html

[52] Email to the authors from David Webber, June 2003.

[53] http://www.quotationspage.com/quotes/Arthur_C._Clarke/

[54] "Is the Information Revolution Dead?," W. Brian Arthur, *Business 2.0,* March 2002.

[55] "The Architecture revolution," Computer Sciences Corporation, Leading Edge Forum Report, August 2003, http://www.csc.com/lef

[56] Rowan, W., *Net Benefit: Guaranteed Electronic Markets,* Macmillan Press, 1999, http://www.atomisedmarkets.com/

[57] *ibid.*

[58] Critical Infrastructure Assurance Office (CIAO), http://www.caio.gov

[59] Rowan, W., Net Benefit: Guaranteed Electronic Markets, Macmillan Press, 1999.

[60] Anderson, M., "Article of Faith," *The Ottawa Citizen,* June 26, 2003.

[61] Arthur, W. B., "Is the Information Revolution Dead?," *Business 2.0,* March 2002.

[62] http://www.gartner.com/DisplayDocument?doc_cd=114867

[63] *ibid.*

[64] Email to the authors from Rajiv Gupta, June 2003.

[65] Discussion during BPMI.org members meeting #10

[66] Strassmann, P., Letter to the Editor, in "Does IT Matter? An HBR Debate," *Harvard Business Review,* June 2003.

[67] Faber, D., "The end of IT as we know it?," *ZDNet Tech Update,* May 28, 2003.

[68] "The Architecture rEvolution," Computer Sciences Corporation, Leading Edge Forum Report, August 2003, http://www.csc.com/lef

[69] George F. Colony, "Forrester CEO looks above IT iceberg waterline," Forrester Research, June 2003.

[70] Interview with Geoffrey Moore, "The Age of Outsourcing", CSC World, http://www.csc.com/features/2003/15.shtml

[71] George F. Colony, "Forrester CEO looks above IT iceberg waterline," Forrester Research, June 2003.

[72] Lepeak, Stan, "Procurement's Future: Outsourcing?," *Line56.com,* August 20, 2002.

[73] Smith, H., Fingar, P., "The New Look and Feel of Outsourcing", from *Business Process Management: The Third Wave,* Meghan-Kiffer Press, 2003, http://www.bpm3.com

[74] "Does IT Matter? An HBR Debate," *Harvard Business Review,* June 2003.

[75] Remarks by Alan Greenspan, Chairman of the Federal Reserve Board, At the U.S. Department of Labor and American Enterprise Institute Conference, Washington, D.C. October 23, 2002.

[76] Galli, P., "Gates Speaks to CEOs," eWEEK, May 21, 2003, http://www.eweek.com/print_article/0,3668,a=42237,00.asp

[77] http://www.informationweek.com/shared/printableArticle.jhtml?articleID=12800359

[78] Email to the authors from Bradley Wheeler, July 2003.
[79] Colony, George F., "Naked Technology," http://www.forrester.com/Info/0,1503,287,FF.html
[80] Spanyi, Andrew, Business Process Management is a Team Sport: Play it to Win!, Anclote Press, 2003. (www.anclote.com)
[81] Rummler, G.A., Brache, A.P., Improving Performance: How to Manage the White Space on the Organization Chart, Jossey-Bass, 1990.
[82] http://www3.gartner.com/pages/story.php.id.8804.s.8.jsp
[83] Smith, H., Fingar, P., "BPM's Third Wave: From Modeling to Management", ebizq.net, http://eai.ebizq.net/bpm/bpm3_1.html
[84] The McKinsey Quarterly, 2002 Number 2, Just-in-Time Strategy for a Turbulent World.
[85] Lepeak, Stan, "Procurement's Future: Outsourcing?," *Line56.com,* August 20, 2002.
[86] Lohr, S., "The Tech Rebound That Isn't Quite," *New York Times,* June 23, 2003.
[87] Sinur J., Thompson, J., "The Business Process Management Scenario: Strategy, Trends and Tactics," Gartner, June 2003.
[88] Vaas, L., "IT Losing Steam,", *eWEEK,* June 2, 2003.
[89] http://www.weforum.org/
[90] Champy, James A., *X-Engineering the Corporation,* Hodder and Stoughton, 2002.
[91] Champy, James A., "X-treme Business Reengineering," *Optimize* magazine, March, 2002.
[92] Email to the authors from David Webber, July 2003.
[93] "Starting Over With BPM," *Line56,* Thursday, May 29, 2003.
[94] Andrews, P., "IT does matter; fixing it might just convince us," *Seattle Times,* June 23 2003.
[95] Rooney. P., "Gates: Microsoft will invest $6.8 Billion in FY '04 On Longhorn Collaboration", *CRN,* July 24, 2003.
[96] Lohr, S., "The Tech Rebound That Isn't Quite," *New York Times,* June 23, 2003.
[97] Interview with Nicholas G. Carr, *Manyworlds,* Summer 2003.
[98] "Does IT Matter? An HBR Debate," *Harvard Business Review,* June 2003.
[99] http://www.ideafinder.com/resource/archives/wow-duell.htm
[100] "Does IT Matter? An HBR Debate," *Harvard Business Review,* June 2003.
[101] *ibid.*
[102] Anderson, M., "Article of Faith," *The Ottawa Citizen,* June 26, 2003.
[103] Arthur, W. B., "Is the Information Revolution Dead?," *Business 2.0,* March 2002. http://www.business2.com/articles/mag/0,1640,37570,00.html
[104] Melymuka, K., "IT Does So Matter!," *Computerworld,* July 7, 2003
[105] Anderson, M., "Article of Faith," *The Ottawa Citizen,* June 26, 2003.

[106] Lohr, S., "The Tech Rebound That Isn't Quite", *New York Times,* June 23, 2003.

[107] Lohr, S., "Is technology business still a growth industry?", New York Times, May 17, 2003, re-printed in the *International Herald Tribune.*

[108] Vogelstein, F., "There's Life Left in the Valley," *FORTUNE,* June 23, 2003.

[109] Rooney. P., "Gates: Microsoft will invest $6.8 Billion in FY '04 On Longhorn Collaboration", *CRN,* July 24, 2003.

[110] Spanyi, Andrew, *Business Process Management is a Team Sport: Play it to Win!,* Meghan-Kiffer Press, 2003. (www.anclote.com)

[111] "Starting Over With BPM," *Line56,* Thursday, May 29, 2003.

[112] *ibid.*

[113] *ibid.*

[114] Email to the authors from John Jainschigg, July 2003.

[115] Email to the authors from Barbara Belon, July 2003.

[116] "Starting Over With BPM," Line56, Thursday, May 29, 2003.

[117] Post, D., Brown, B., "On The Horizon: Let's Talk Jump-Starts, Not Caution," *Information Week,* July 7, 2003.

[118] Follow-up to the semiannual monetary policy report to the Congress. Testimony before the Committee on Financial Services, U.S. House of Representatives, April 30, 2003.

[119] http://www.memecentral.com/

[120] Schussel, G., "What, Me Worry? You Bet!," *eWEEK,* July 7, 2003.

[121] http://cio.com/archive/071503/reloaded.html

[122] "IT Reloaded", Q&A with economist W. Brian Arthur, *CIO Magazine,* July 15, 2003

[123] *ibid.*

[124] Email to the authors from Bradley Wheeler, July 2003.

[125] Email to the authors from Ajit Kapoor, July 2003.

[126] Venkatraman, V., "Other Voices: The Real Impact of IT Is Just Beginning," *InformationWeek,* June 23, 2003.

[127] http://www.infoeconomics.com/

[128] Strassmann, P. A., Letter to the Editor, *Harvard Business Review,* June 2003.

[129] http://www.alinean.com/HBR_PS.asp and "Who's Getting ROI from IT Spending?" Alinean Research.

[130] Hayes, F., "IT Delivers," *Computerworld,* May 19, 2003.

[131] Kirkpatrick, D., "Stupid-Journal Alert; Why HBR's View of Tech Is Dangerous," *FORTUNE,* May 27, 2003.

[132] Lashinsky, A., "Tech Matters. So what?," *CNNMoney,* May 28, 2003.

[133] Evans, B., "Business Technology: IT Doesn't Matter?," *InformationWeek,* May 12, 2003.

[134] Evans, B., "Business Technology: IT Is A Must, No Matter How You

View It," *InformationWeek,* May 19, 2003.
135 Whiting, R., "CIOs Sure Think IT Matters," *InformationWeek,* May 23, 2003.
136 Keefe, P., "IT Does Matter," *ComputerWorld,* May 12, 2003.
137 Melymuka, K., "Get Over Yourself: The Pervasiveness of IT may be making it strategically irrelevant," *Computerworld,* May 12, 2003.
138 Melymuka, K., "IT Does So Matter!,", *Computerworld,* July 7, 2003.
139 Wallace, R., "Intel's Barrett fires back in IT relevance debate," *EETimes,* May 15, 2003.
140 Maney, K., "How IBM, Dell managed to build crushing tech dominance," *USAToday,* May 20, 2003.
141 Broadbent, M., McGee, K., McDonald, M., "IT Success Requires Discipline and Innovation," Gartner, FT-20-0693, May 12, 2003.
142 http://www.johnhagel.com/blog20030515.html
143 http://weblog.infoworld.com/dickerson/2003/06/02.html